Food Crops
vs. Feed Crops

Food Crops vs. Feed Crops

Global Substitution of Grains in Production

David Barkin
Rosemary L. Batt
Billie R. DeWalt

Lynne Rienner Publishers • Boulder and London

Published in the United States of America in 1990
by Lynne Rienner Publishers, Inc.
1800 30th Street, Boulder, Colorado 80301

and in the United Kingdom by
Lynne Rienner Publishers, Inc.
3 Henrietta Street, Covent Garden, London WC2E 8LU

Library of Congress Cataloging-in-Publication Data
Barkin, David.
    Food crops vs. feed crops: the global substitution of grains in production/by
David Barkin, Rosemary L. Batt, Billie R. DeWalt.
        p. cm.
    Includes bibliographical references.
    ISBN 1-55587-185-2
    1. Food supply—Developing countries. 2. Malnutrition—Developing
countries. 3. Grain trade—Developing countries. 4. Grain as feed—
Developing countries. 5. Animal industry—Developing countries.
I. Batt, Rosemary L. II. DeWalt, Billie R. III. Title.
HD9018.D44B37 1990
338.1'91724—dc20   89–24364
                                                        CIP

British Cataloguing in Publication Data
A Cataloguing in Publication record for this book
is available from the British Library.

Printed and bound in the United States of America

The paper used in this publication meets the requirements
of the American National Standard for Permanence of
Paper for Printed Library Materials Z39.48–1984.

*For
Benjamin, Ron,
Saara, and Gareth*

Contents

Preface

The genesis of our research project came long before we started the collaborative effort that led to this book. The project has its roots in a series of field studies and analyses of the evolution of agricultural production in Mexico and Central America. In addition, we have been stimulated by the work of many other scholars in diverse fields.

For a long time, David Barkin has been advocating the need to examine the impact on people's lives of national integration into the world economy. His analysis is an extension of the seminal work by Steven Hymer (in the United States) and Christian Palloix (in France) that obliged many people to reexamine the dynamics of the international economy. In the early 1970s it was still too soon for most people in Mexico to recognize the powerful influence that the actors in the world market were exerting on policymaking and the decisions of individual producers. Some people were beginning to become aware of the way in which this process was affecting consumption patterns and even life-styles; but the shrill analyses of the moment were dismissed by the orthodox as simplistic Marxism, while the burgeoning middle classes anxiously struggled to embrace the many forms of "coca-colonialism," as the process was dubbed in the literature.

Barkin's work in this area has been a result of joint research projects sponsored by the Universidad Autónoma Metropolitana, Xochimilco Campus (UAM-X), and the Ecodevelopment Center (CECODES), a multidisciplinary organization created under the aegis of Mexico's National Science and Technology Council (CONACYT). These studies documented the ways in which individual producers and their communities, as well as policymakers in the halls of national power, were all being compelled to consider events and pressures originating beyond the national frontiers, forces that were unknown to, or misunderstood by, the actors. Barkin's analysis of the influence of international economic forces on the rapidly changing structure of agricultural production in Mexico, and that of other Latin American colleagues examining the same phenomenon, have gradually been integrated into the conventional understanding of Mexican rural society. By the early 1980s it became virtually impossible to describe the evolution of Mexican agriculture without acknowledging the commanding influence of the international economy.

At about the same time, Billie R. DeWalt was conducting anthropological field studies of the evolution of rural societies, first in Mexico and then in Honduras. Unlike anthropological studies that focus solely on social and cultural processes within small communities, his work (modeled on that of such scholars as Eric Wolf, Sidney Mintz, and Pertti Pelto) sought to understand how local communities were being affected by their articulation with larger regional, national, and international spheres. This work convinced him of how destructive these larger forces could be to the social and ecological organization of rural production.

Much of DeWalt's research was carried out while he participated in the International Sorghum and Millet Collaborative Research Support Program (INTSORMIL—a consortium working with the International Agricultural Research Centers to improve the world agricultural situation). He and other researchers at the University of Kentucky were attempting to incorporate social concerns into generation of new technology and agricultural development.

It soon became clear that combining Barkin's mostly macrolevel work on the changing nature of agricultural production in Mexico and DeWalt's mostly microlevel work on the changing nature of agricultural communities would be productive. Beginning in 1983 and financed jointly by our home institutions, with outside support from INTSORMIL and the United Nations University, we conducted field studies, in a wide variety of regions in rural Mexico, on the socioeconomic impacts of technological change and the substitution of grains.

As we were working with the results of our years of research in Mexico, and the deepening crisis that was developing with peculiar twists in the rural areas, it became apparent that similar problems were occurring throughout the food-producing regions of the Third World. At the same time, the leading research organizations of the international development community still were not demonstrating concern that agricultural modernization might be threatening the welfare of small farmers and even the viability of their communities. Advocates of the alternative development approaches ("small is beautiful," basic needs, appropriate technology, farming systems research, sustainability, etc.) that place these issues at the top of their agendas have been unable to influence reorientation of priorities in the major international agricultural development and research organizations.

We decided to undertake a quantitative study of the displacement of food grains by feed grains as part of an effort to lay the groundwork for further national studies of its socioeconomic impacts. We were convinced that the proponents of agricultural modernization, because they are committed to unrealistic models of economic behavior, could not understand the position of defenders of small-scale farming communities. The research for this book was undertaken to try to demonstrate that an alternative approach to understanding trends in world grain production and trade is necessary. In spite of the unorthodoxy of our approach, we gained a responsive hearing at the Rockefeller Foundation, where Joyce Moock and Robert Herdt assisted us in securing support.

We were particularly fortunate in being able to recruit Rosemary L. Batt to collaborate with us. A former student of DeWalt, Batt was then trying to extend her anthropological work and training to acquire an understanding of the dynamics of the world economy. She offered to return to Mexico and participate in data preparation and analysis. As a result, we were able to build a valuable data bank on production and trade in basic agricultural commodities that is now at the disposal of other researchers in Mexico.

None of us realized the time that would be required to complete the tedious chore of transforming the enormous volume of raw data into the series of country and regional analyses presented in this book. Batt accomplished this task while assiduously finding and assimilating myriad tomes of country studies as we wended our way toward a final manuscript. Batt is now on a MacArthur Fellowship pursuing doctoral research in urban studies and planning at the Massachusetts Institute of

Technology.

Our work would have been many times more difficult had it not been for the generous support of the International Maize and Wheat Improvement Center (CIMMYT), which provided CECODES with magnetic versions (on diskettes) of the data banks on production and trade from the Food and Agricultural Organization (FAO) in Rome. CIMMYT also extended to us its legendary hospitality when we sought to avail ourselves of its extensive library collection and discuss our concerns and findings with the staff.

During the studies that preceded this effort, we enjoyed the generous collaboration of numerous individuals and institutions. We must especially mention for their contributions Adolfo Chávez, a division chief at the National Nutrition Institute in Mexico, and Mercedes Hernández, who worked directly with us in field studies; Iván Restrepo, director of CECODES, and Blanca Suárez, long-time collaborator with Barkin at CECODES and director of some of our field studies; and Sergio Reyes Luján, general rector, and Francisco José Paoli, rector, of UAM-X. The enthusiastic support offered by UAM-X's Departments of Economics, Agronomy, and Social Medicine allowed students performing their social service obligations to participate in our research as field assistants; José Carlos Escudero and Guillermo Pérez Jerónimo of UAM joined us in designing and implementing some of the early field studies that served as background for the present work; Kathleen M. DeWalt helped us to design those aspects of our projects focusing on nutrition and health and collaborated with us in the field research; and Nevin Scrimshaw, former vice-rector of the United Nations University, helped us to obtain funding for one of our projects and continues to offer encouragement for our efforts.

Thanks to Anne Parrish, who assisted in the completion of the manuscript, and to Teresa Epperson, whose good humor and ability served well in the preparation of the final version of the tables.

We would also like to acknowledge the very useful suggestions of Fred J. Ruppel; the keen editorial job done by Pam Ferdinand; and the prompt, courteous, and efficient production job of Gia Hamilton and the staff at Lynne Rienner Publishers.

Most books are the culmination of a long process of research, thinking, and writing. That is certainly true of this effort. In handing the manuscript over to the publishers, however, we also have the hope that it is just a beginning, that the suggestive results presented here will spark other investigators further to explore the causes and results of the substitution of grains in a representative sample of countries around the world.

In the course of our analysis of the data on a country-by-country basis, we solicited and received help from a great many people and organizations who offered information and assistance on developments in their countries. Although their contributions are far too numerous to list here, these contacts offered us constant reassurance that it would be possible to coordinate a series of case studies conducted by national research teams in each country, which would contribute to a better understanding of the welfare implications of agricultural modernization. It is to these people that we dedicate this book, in the hope that it will contribute to redirecting more efforts to strengthening the production of grain for food in the less developed countries.

Food Crops
vs. Feed Crops

1

The Substitution of Grains
in World Production

Ending hunger is the hidden agenda of this book. Our previous studies in Mexico (Barkin and Suárez 1985; Barkin 1987; Barkin and DeWalt 1988) demonstrated that the substitution of grains in production is associated with impoverishment of the rural economy and with food shortages on the national level. Other studies (many of which are cited here) have confirmed that substitution in production among grains is common, and that this process is often associated with growing inequality of access to food; the middle classes and wealthy eat an increasingly rich diet, while undernutrition and malnutrition are common in poor farming communities and urban slums throughout the Third World.

In undertaking the research reported here, our concern was to determine whether further study of our underlying premises is warranted in other countries. We are now persuaded that detailed country, community, and commodity case studies of the sort conducted in Mexico would be fruitful, not simply to document the relation among grain substitution, impoverishment, and malnutrition, but also to evaluate the wisdom of existing policies of agricultural modernization.

We examine in this book one aspect of the commercialization, or modernization, of agriculture in food-producing regions of the Third World. Our Mexican research showed that the extraordinary success of agricultural modernization—leading to huge increases in the output of feed for animals, as well as of higher valued crops for urban markets and export—was accompanied by a growing inability to produce basic foodstuffs. As similar developments have occurred around

1

the world, economists often hail this transition as evidence of sectoral development. The international development community has encouraged and hastened the process by providing financial and technical assistance and political support for governments embracing this approach; in contrast, regimes more concerned with achieving food self-sufficiency are severely criticized and occasionally even transformed into pariahs in the world market economy.

We do not expect to resolve the conflict between the advocates of food self-sufficiency and the proponents of comparative advantage. Rather, we wish to contribute to a more balanced assessment of the issues raised by the worldwide tendency to move toward specialization in nonfood crops. Our case studies suggest that an extreme solution—exclusive reliance on cash crops or food crops—is not in the best interests of people in most regions. The balance, however, currently rests on the side of commercialization of agriculture, especially the production of feed for livestock or cash crops for export.

Commercialization is occurring as part of internationalization, of the process of integrating national economies into the world market and facilitating the intrusion of global price structures, production systems, and consumption patterns into local decisionmaking processes (Barkin 1982, 1985). Some producers in the Third World are rapidly adapting to the new imperatives of international standardization that national governments feel obliged to accelerate by aligning relative price structures in local markets with international patterns. Commercialization frequently expands at the expense of food output, eroding the national food-producing capacity. Subsistence food production persists only because the poverty of its practitioners precludes alternatives.

Our book uses global figures on the substitution of grains in production to document a worrisome trend in the world grain economy: Third World countries everywhere are becoming more dependent on imports to assure basic food supplies for their people. There are a few notable exceptions to this tendency, worthy of further study but generally belittled by the international community—mocked by being tossed together with the case studies of extreme poverty suffered by traditional producers engaged in minimalist survival strategies or of governments that pursue expensive and/or ineffectual populist strategies of food self-sufficiency.

Although this book addresses the problem of substitution of

grains, the underlying issue is the ability of people to feed themselves. Orthodox economists often evade such problems; they advocate rational policies that are supposed to promote efficient production systems and call on the market to assure adequate supplies of goods for each participant in the society. Such approaches assume that by developing an efficient productive system, more goods will be available and everyone will be able to participate. In the real world, however, large groups of people cannot depend on the market to supply them with their basic necessities: For want of money, they cannot exercise the "effective demand" that would allow them to acquire these commodities. As a result, vast numbers of people must rely on their own production, and that of their neighbors, for any goods they are to consume. A decline in people's ability to produce their own food grains, in this setting, often means a reduction in their nutritional standards.

Commercial production of feed grains, it is sometimes argued, offers an alternative for improving economic conditions in rural areas. With fertilizers, technical assistance, more productive seeds, and credit, producers can buy their basic foodstuffs with the proceeds from crop sales and still have sufficient income to purchase other commodities. The logic appears unassailable, but reality is often treacherous: Traditional foods are frequently not available in local markets, and when they are, their cost is often beyond the means of poor families; modern food substitutes are expensive; crop failures leave small-scale producers with unmanageable debts or actually force them off their land; markets become saturated and/or prices for feed grains decline unexpectedly. The list of problems appears endless, especially to small-scale producers who often must face monopoly structures in the markets where they purchase inputs, borrow money, or sell crops.

As we see the problem, the substitution of feed for food grains frequently sets the stage for problems of immiseration and/or malnutrition. Farming communities that assume responsibility for sowing the nation's basic foodstuffs are usually not the principal beneficiaries of agricultural modernization schemes. With the shift in cropping patterns, not only are resources moved from food to feed grain production, but a new group of producers enters the grain scene. The social organization of production is itself transformed: The new crop is generally sold for cash and often involves the introduction of hybrid or improved seed varieties with new production processes. Planting of cash crops is frequently financed by loans, further removing the possibility of participation for farmers who grow food for their own subsistence or for sale in local markets.

Substitution does not occur spontaneously. It is a direct response to an interrelated series of events in international and national markets and domestic policy circles. With the generalization of international markets, changes in relative prices, and the spread of new agricultural technologies, it is becoming increasingly difficult for small-scale farming communities to supply grains at prices competitive with those prevailing on world markets: Export subsidies, cheap production credit, and economies of scale confer a huge advantage to farmers in the advanced countries. When such advantages are combined with export promotion (e.g., a Commodity Credit Corporation) and food aid programs that often deliver food to poor countries with no budgetary outlays (the costs are simply added to the country's foreign debt, which will then have to be confronted by a future administration), it appears miraculous (and irrational) that *any* basic food staples are produced by small farming communities in the less developed nations. As a result, a new international division of agricultural production has emerged: The advanced industrial countries of the North have become the world's granary.

This international environment exercises a powerful influence on national policymaking throughout the Third World. With cheap food grains available on world markets, often on concessional terms, policymakers promote export crops and feed grains for domestic (and export) livestock production. Such apparently "developmental" policies underlie the form that agricultural modernization takes. This pattern of development is not socially neutral: The participants in the evolving agricultural economies of the Third World are the new rural elites, groups whose very success is making it increasingly difficult for small-scale farmers to survive by producing traditional food grains. The majority of farmers in these countries find their economic conditions deteriorating.

The dilemma facing the Third World nations today is how to promote a form of agricultural modernization that does not impoverish the majority of their farmers. What policies can assure farmers and their countries the ability to feed themselves? This question provoked our research; the resulting book shows simply that dozens of less developed countries are, in fact, facing such a dilemma. This apparently straightforward problem still is a point of considerable controversy among influential segments of the development community. We feel it is important to document this substitution of feed for food grains in order to convince both students of these problems and policymakers to undertake the difficult task of conducting detailed country case studies of this process. Such studies are necessary to design the specific macro- and microlevel programs that will strengthen the food-producing capabilities of each nation as part of a broader program to support a mass-based effort to alleviate poverty and improve nutritional standards. Our case studies of the Mexican experience offer a model that other country teams may consider in attempting to understand the relationship between changes in productive structures and socioeconomic development.

PURPOSES OF THE BOOK

The attainment of food self-sufficiency has been a major goal of most developing countries over the past 25 years. Many of these countries have formulated national-level food policies or a constellation of production, trade, and consumption policies specifically aimed at improving food self-sufficiency—that is, the capacity to meet the food needs of the bulk of the population. Yet, research on world food security and self-sufficiency shows two contradictory processes: On the one hand, food production has kept pace with, and frequently exceeded, the population growth rate in developing countries during the period 1961–1986 (Paulino 1986). Government's subsidizing of irrigation works and agricultural inputs has helped improve output and productivity both through the expansion of acreage under cultivation and through technology-based improvements in yields. On the other hand, food dependency as measured by the growth in value of net food imports has skyrocketed during this same period. Latin American and sub-Saharan African countries that were once net food exporters are now net importers.

Our current study documents this pattern of increased food production and food dependency, based on data on grain production between 1961 and 1986. We focus on grain production because cereals account for the bulk of global caloric and protein intake. Grains constitute 83% of the food crop production of developing countries and accounted for 87% of the growth in food production between 1960 and 1980 (Paulino 1986:17–18). Thus, trends in grain production and trade are the key to understanding changes in worldwide food production and consumption patterns.

Why has increased per capita food production not led to improved food self-sufficiency in most countries? A common explanation is that these countries are experiencing economic development (Huddleston 1987:226). As a result, per capita income is rising, the standard of living of the majority of the population is improving, and people can afford to buy foods in greater quantities and of greater diversity and quality. In other words, increasing imports reflect the fact that domestic food production cannot keep pace with the consumption demand occasioned by increasing incomes. Although this argument is persuasive and may explain partially the growing food gap, comparisons of per capita food production and income represent a first, relatively crude measure of the world food situation and developing countries' economic welfare. This explanation does not, for example, take into consideration the way in which increasing food production has been accompanied by major substitutions of grains in production and consumption.

Our book offers a quantitative examination of the major trends in worldwide grain production, consumption, and trade during the past 25 years. It covers 24 developing countries, the USSR, and the developed market economies as a group. The countries account for 86% of total area and 88% of world production in cereals. The focus of the research, however, is on developing countries. Our purposes are:

To identify and describe the changes in food production and trade in selected developing countries since 1960;

To analyze these production trends in relation to the changing grain trade in these countries;

To explain the increasing dependency on food imports, despite the efforts of national governments and bilateral and multilateral aid agencies, of developing countries; and

To provide an initial analysis of these issues to serve as the basis for future intensive case studies that will explore the distributional and broader socioeconomic impacts of changes in grain production and trade in the selected developing countries.

Our approach to the food question grows out of our previous work that examined Mexico's transition to food dependency. The country's initial attainment of food self-sufficiency during the

1950s was a consequence of agrarian reform efforts that brought about the expansion of smallholder production of maize, the traditional food crop both for local consumption and for sale in national markets. At the same time, the substantial investments in technological development in Mexico led to the green revolution in wheat that created the basis for significant increases in yields and acreage in production. Similar successful technological improvements in the United States contributed to Mexico's second green revolution in sorghum (DeWalt 1985a), which has erupted dramatically after 1958. Our detailed study of the evolution of the grain sector in Mexico shows that wheat and sorghum (for feed)—both oriented toward urban middle and upper income markets—have displaced land dedicated to the production of maize and beans. This substitution of grains in production both reflects and has occasioned profound changes in many facets of society (Barkin 1981; DeWalt and Barkin 1985; Barkin and Suárez 1985; Barkin and DeWalt 1988).

These changes in productivity and production accompanied and accelerated Mexico's economic development. Substantial improvements in per capita consumption standards were the result of the agrarian reform that allowed formerly landless rural laborers to become successful producers of maize and other food crops. Later, the technological developments occasioned by the creation of dwarf wheat varieties made possible a dramatic change in cropping systems: Maize production by smallholders in central Mexico gave way to wheat production by large-scale agriculturalists in the northwest, who had privileged access to irrigation and other infrastructure as well as the financial backing to incorporate the new technology rapidly into production (Barkin and Suárez 1985). The new varieties of wheat required processing in new capital-intensive mills constructed by large enterprises that supplanted the established smaller firms. Similarly, the introduction of new hybrid sorghum varieties into Mexico by the private farming community came at a propitious moment: Many farmers with their own sources of credit and equipment were searching for profitable alternatives to maize. They found in the new grain a way of circumventing the growing encroachment of government in agriculture while increasing profits and easing the job of administering their businesses—sorghum production required far fewer people-days of labor and could easily be mechanized. The animal feed companies competed vigorously with each other in offering attractive incentives for farmers to deliver their harvests.

Our studies of this process identified the substantial changes that these interrelated events have had on Mexican society. We traced their impact on the transformation of production and consumption, and their uneven distributional impacts on producers, rural workers, and consumers, and on different regions in Mexico. Even as the outward signs of national integration became more apparent with the establishment of schools, rural clinics, and government stores to improve basic food distribution at fair prices, the family structure was being torn asunder, and new generations were finding little opportunity to become productively employed. We documented how the substitution of grains in production contributed to the idling of land in many rainfed agricultural areas, and to a dramatic resurgence of dependency on external markets for basic food crops. These shifts exacerbated the already highly concentrated distribution of personal income in rural Mexico and promoted an increase in migratory flows to urban areas and to the United States.

The overall goal of the present study is to contribute to an understanding of the implications for producer and consumer welfare of the changing composition of grain production, trade, and consumption in the societies of developing countries between 1960 and 1985. This time period corresponds to: (1) profound changes occurring in world grain markets, with many developing countries becoming net importers; (2) the introduction of modern varieties of rice, wheat, and hybrid maize and sorghum in several important developing countries; and (3) the development decades, proclaimed by the United Nations, that have resulted in substantial investment in agriculture by foundations and bilateral and multilateral agencies and banks. These three elements have been accompanied by dynamic changes in the grains that are produced, who is producing them, and the purposes for which they are produced.

ANALYTICAL PERSPECTIVES

Our work in Mexico showed that a similar trend toward the substitution of grains in production was occurring throughout the Western Hemisphere (DeWalt 1985b). We found that feed crops for animals were displacing food crops for people, and that there was a move from labor-intensive products to mechanized farming wherever practicable. Food dependency, when measured by net grain imports, was increasing in many countries.

The most frequent pattern of substitution of grains in production documented here is the displacement of "traditional" food grains, grown by small producers, by "nontraditional" grains grown by larger-scale enterprises for higher income markets, industrial uses (feed), and export.

In the literature, there are radically different kinds of approaches to understanding the dramatic changes that have occurred in the adoption and diffusion of crops throughout the world. One approach comes from the biological and agricultural sciences: that crops always do better outside of their area of origin and domestication. The argument is that in a totally new ecological setting, plants do not have to contend with the insect pests, diseases, and other pathogens with which they have evolved (Jennings and Cock 1977). They can thus express close to their full yield potential without being hampered by environmental constraints. A second, related, explanation is that modern varieties and hybrids adapted to a variety of ecological settings have become available, and that, because of their higher yields, they are able to replace other cultigens (e.g., much of the literature on the green revolution). Researchers often view these two factors as sufficient to explain the rapid transformation of cropping patterns observed in developing countries.

A second approach focuses strictly on the relative economic profitability of crops. According to this line of reasoning, producers will adopt cultivation of the most profitable commodity. Countries, or regions within countries, expand production in the commodities for which they have a comparative advantage, depending upon the particular mix of natural and human resources and available capital (Leamer 1984). This explanation assumes that the free market mechanism will adjust prices according to market supply and demand; agriculturalists will be induced to produce the most profitable crop until the relative profit margins for all crops are equal. This process depends on "getting prices right" (Timmer 1986), but government intervention frequently disrupts the market mechanism. According to this line of thinking, governments should intervene in the market only when prices have been distorted for political or institutional reasons.

The approach used in this book relates the agronomic characteristics of crops to economic and social factors (Wolf 1982; Barkin and DeWalt 1988). While the biological characteristics of plants may establish their potential for high yields, and profitability calculations play a central role in the adoption and diffusion of crops, these are not the only factors that influence the decisionmaking of producers. Our central premise is that the introduction and spread of nontraditional grains in a region or country depends upon the relative distribution of resources in the society, the role the government plays in promoting the adoption of nontraditional grains, and the extent to which the country is integrated into world commodity markets—and accepts international grain prices as the basis for determining national prices. That is, while the availability of nontraditional grains may provide the opportunity for growing crops with higher yields, profitability will depend on market prices relative to the cost of inputs, both of which are highly influenced by government policies and grain markets in both developed and developing countries. Farmers will tend to adopt more profitable crops wherever possible, but farmers are not a homogeneous group: Some are better positioned to take advantage of the promotion of nontraditional and more profitable crops than are others.

The process of crop substitution can take place in at least three different but possibly interrelated ways. First, it can be demand-driven in the sense that market prices and/or technology induce or oblige consumers to purchase a different set of goods for their own use, for animal feeds, or other purposes. Second, the process may be input-driven so that producers are encouraged to change their crop so as to take advantage of, or use more of, new technologies or production techniques. Third, the changes may be labor process—driven in that producers may change crops so as more easily to mechanize, or in other ways to displace labor or ease the management task. Ultimately, through these mechanisms, the profitability of the crop improves, and some producers are able to take advantage of the increased profitability.

With the increasing integration of developing countries into world commodity markets, we would expect to find a corresponding tendency toward the substitution of grains in production: Cereal food crops historically produced and consumed locally would give way to commercial production of grain destined for other uses. In regions where noncereal food crops are significant in traditional systems of production and consumption, we would expect that these crops would also decline relative to commercially oriented agriculture.

We would also expect the substitution of grains in production to be accompanied by two major trends in trade: increased exports of agricultural commodities and increased imports of basic foodstuffs by developing countries to compensate for the relative decline in domestic food production. On the one hand, the growth in the export of agricultural commodities responds to political pressures and economic imperatives to earn foreign exchange to contribute to the country's balance of payments, to make it better prepared to negotiate its debts or to face its international obligations. It is also the result of individual producers' decisions to cultivate more profitable export crops. On the other hand, the growing net imports of food may drain those same foreign earnings and leave the country in a more precarious economic situation while decreasing its food self-sufficiency and food security.

METHODOLOGY

Our approach to understanding food production and consumption represents a departure from many contemporary studies of global food problems in at least three fundamental ways. First, rather than analyze data on a global, continental level, we review production and trade trends on a country-by-country basis. This methodological approach is significant because it provides the opportunity to identify in-country patterns that are often masked when data are aggregated across different countries or continents. Second, rather than looking simply at aggregate production figures, we analyze shifts in production and trade of individual grains within each country. This level of detail is particularly important because countries vary greatly in their uses of different grains: Maize is primarily a food crop in many sub-Saharan African countries, but a feed crop in northern Africa. Sorghum and millet are food crops in some African and Asian countries, but feed crops in most Latin American countries. Although maize is the primary human staple of most Latin American countries, it is generally used for feed in Argentina. By combining analyses of individual countries with analyses of individual grains within those countries, we are better able to assess the meaning of trends in shifting grain production identified through quantitative data. Third, our research seeks to comprehend changes in food self-sufficiency not only with respect to their impact on a nation's consumers and on its balance of trade but, equally or more importantly, their differential impact on food producers, who still constitute the bulk of the population in most developing countries. What, for example, do major shifts in agricultural production mean for the livelihood of small-scale producers of food crops, when contrasted to those who cultivate export products, or to urban consumers?

This book contributes to existing literature on world food issues by focusing on the substitution of grains in production and the distributional impacts of this process on producers as well as consumers. By the substitution of grains in production, we mean that the share of one or more grains in a country's overall production is increasing relative to other grains. We document that major substitutions of grains in production are occurring in developing countries throughout the world. The primary pattern that emerges from quantitative data on grain production and trade is that staple cereals, traditionally produced by small-scale farmers for themselves and for most of their neighbors to consume, are being displaced by grains produced commercially for animal feed, for sale in middle and upper income markets, and for export. This process of substitution of grains in production has occurred most dramatically in Latin America, but also in several African and Asian countries. By analyzing these patterns in the changing composition of grain production in countries throughout the developing world, we hope to identify the source of uneven distribution of the benefits of increased food production. Our aim is to develop an alternative explanation for why developing countries are simultaneously increasing food production and food dependency—an explanation that can be further explored in detailed case studies on the countries we survey in this book.

The years 1961–1986 correspond to the period when developing countries dramatically increased their participation in world commodity markets and span the time during which the International Agricultural Research Centers achieved substantial success with the dissemination of high yielding varieties of wheat, rice, maize, and sorghum. The resulting green revolution has led to the modernization of production, the modification of cropping patterns, and unprecedented increases in output. These years also cover the period during which there has been substantial promotion of agricultural development by foundations, bilateral and multilateral agencies, and banks.

Our primary data cover 25 years of area, yield, production, and trade figures for the eight major cereal grains in the world—rice, wheat, maize, sorghum, millet, barley, oats, and rye. These data are derived from those prepared by the FAO of the United Nations. For most countries, in-country data has also been analyzed and compared to the FAO data; where discrepancies exist between the bodies of data, their implications are discussed. For countries and regions of the world where noncereal food crops (such as roots, tubers, and legumes) play a central role in the food system, we analyze trends in production, consumption, and trade.

The study is based on an examination of trends in each country. To identify the substitution of grains in production, we realize a number of interrelated analyses:

We first examine the *recent historical pattern of grain utilization* in the selected countries to determine whether each grain is used for direct human consumption, for animal feed or other industrial uses, or for export. We also determine, wherever possible, who are the major producers and producing regions for the most important grains.

We analyze, for each country, the *changes in land utilization for each grain* between 1961 and 1986, and calculate the rate of growth in land utilization for each crop.

We compare *yield data* to the changes in area for each crop to determine, in a general way, how the introduction of technological change has affected the cropping systems within each country.

We use available secondary sources to identify *changes in the dominant work processes* for the various grains under production. This bringing together of quantitative and qualitative materials is important to evaluate the impact of modifications in the cropping patterns on the employment and income distribution of producers. We also use secondary source material to understand the relationship between changes in grain production and the nutritional status of low income producers and consumers.

Finally, we characterize and quantify the *interaction between the evolution of national grain production and the grain trade balance* of each country. We analyze how the changing composition of grain production has turned food self-sufficient or surplus countries into major importers or exporters of food in recent years.

To trace the changing composition of grain production and trade in each country, we computed five-year averages documenting the land use patterns and the structure of output, exports, and imports for each of the grains and for cereals as a whole. Five-year averages were used to reduce the distortions from abnormal years and to focus on overall trends. The 25-year average of the share of cultivated land and production of each crop was also determined along with the average annual growth rates. While the country-by-country analyses tend to focus on those crops that show major changes in area and output, computations for all grains for all countries in the study are presented in the tables at the back of the book.

Countries were chosen for comprehensiveness. For maximum coverage of overall world grain production and trade, the study includes the major grain-producing and exporting countries of Latin America, Asia, and Africa. So as not to bias the study, some small and medium grain producers are also included. This balance improves our ability to comprehend in our analyses a variety of particular economic and historical circumstances. All of the countries (with the exception of the Soviet Union and China, which are included for the sake of completeness) are market economies that are therefore suitable for appraising the explanatory value of our central argument. The selection process permits us to present a rather complete picture of the extent to which the substitution of grains in production is occurring, and it creates a basis for future, more detailed studies of the phenomenon.

Our study covers a minimum of 79% (millet) and a maximum of 95% (sorghum) of the total world area and production of each grain. We summarize this coverage by region for each grain in Table I. The individual country analyses contain relevant data on noncereal crops where such information was pertinent to explain the changing dynamics of food production, consumption, and trade.

There is some important variation in the coverage of cereal crops on a regional basis. The countries we selected in Latin America allowed our data set for this region to be the most complete and consistent, reaching 79% or higher for each cereal but barley (72%). Overall coverage in Africa is weaker: 65% of grain cultivation in general, but only 23% of rice cultivation and 48% of millet area. The study includes 82% of the cultivated cereal land in Asia, but only 59% of barley cultivation.

As mentioned earlier, in contrast to many world food production and consumption studies, which trace patterns of growth by regions of the world, this study includes general regional overviews but also analyzes each country separately. This is necessary because individual grains are produced for different ends, depending upon the country. With rare exceptions, a national-level analysis is required to assess the changing composition of agricultural production and trade as well as the meaning of this change, which is frequently not apparent from data aggregated by world region, continent, or subregion. For example, what may be a staple food crop in one country may be an export crop in another. Thus, to identify trends in staple crop production versus commercial or export-oriented production, individual country studies are necessary.[1]

Finally, our focus on producers as well as consumers is intended to fill a gap in the literature. While the data base for the research is sufficient to examine our central concerns and identify major patterns of change, it only begins to uncover the socioeconomic impacts on producers and consumers, and future case studies are needed to provide more comprehensive understanding.

2

Worldwide Patterns in Grain Production and Trade

The origin and diffusion of the cultivation of staple food crops around the globe is complex: Maize originating in Latin America was introduced to Africa and now covers large areas of that continent; potatoes from Peru went to Europe. Half of the world's population still lives by subsistence production of food staples. Distinct cereals, adapted to particular regional ecologies and climates, still provide the bulk of the world's population with its basic food: rice in Asia; wheat in North America, Europe, the Middle East, and northern Africa; maize in Latin America. In Table II, we present the average global distribution of cultivated grain area and production by region for the 1961–1986 period.

Within continents and even within countries, however, the basic staples vary. While much of black Africa south of the Sahel depends on the production and consumption of sorghum, millet, and maize, for example, wheat is the basic staple in northern Africa. In India, while rice is the basic staple in some regions, sorghum and millet feed the majority of the population in dry regions. An adequate understanding of the modern transformations in agriculture in developing market economies requires an analysis on a country-by-country basis, and frequently on a regional basis within countries. In only a few cases does aggregate data by continents allow us to approach a meaningful understanding of the changes that are occurring. In Table III, we list the current staple cereal crops for each of the countries included; we define the staple cereal grains of each country as those cultivated for producers' direct consumption as well as that of a substantial portion of the domestic population.

17

GRAIN SUBSTITUTION IN PRODUCTION

This study demonstrates that the substitution of grains in production away from food for direct consumption is a worldwide phenomenon. It is also a complex and uneven one: Some countries and regions show a much more advanced level of transformation than do others; some governments have enacted policies specifically designed to stem the process. But it is evident that land dedicated to traditional staple grains is declining relative to overall agricultural production in many countries. Staple cereals for direct human consumption by small-scale producers and the bulk of the population in developing countries are being displaced by higher priced grains oriented toward middle and upper income markets, by grains for industrial uses and for animal feed (to produce meat that is primarily geared toward middle and upper income markets), and by grains for export.

In 13 out of the 24 countries reviewed here, at least 5% of the total land cultivated in grain shows a shift from human cereal production to commercial grain production for other uses in the past 25 years. The countries that have undergone this transformation are, in Latin America: Brazil, Colombia, Mexico, Peru, and Venezuela; in Africa: Egypt, Nigeria, Tanzania, South Africa, and Sudan; in Asia: India, the Philippines, and Thailand. In eight countries (Colombia, Mexico, Peru, Venezuela, Tanzania, South Africa, Thailand, and the Philippines), this substitution has affected 10% or more of the land in grain production.

In two countries—Algeria and Morocco—in which one of the traditional staple food grains is increasing (barley), utilization data suggest that the increase is destined more for feed use than for direct human consumption.

In six countries, the substitution of grains in production is in favor of staple grains to feed the domestic population. Where these changes are occurring, they are usually in response to specific government efforts to attain food self-sufficiency. The countries in this group include Burkina Faso, Kenya, Zimbabwe, Bangladesh, Indonesia, and Turkey. In three of these countries, however—Kenya, Zimbabwe, and Indonesia—one staple food grain is increasing relative to another, with contradictory impacts. In some of these cases, as described below, the substitution of one food grain for another adversely affects a substantial minority of the population.

In three countries—Argentina, Ethiopia, and China—the impact of the substitution of grains in production on food self-sufficiency is not clear or does not appear to be significant.

A summary of the substitution of grains in production for the countries in the study is provided in Table IV. For each country, we show which grains are increasing in area, which are decreasing, and the percentage of the total cultivated grain land shifted out of staple grain production during the 25-year period under review.

The substitution of staple food grains by grains for other uses may or may not correlate with a country's current position with respect to food self-sufficiency, but it is an important contributing factor. Colombia, one of the more self-sufficient countries with respect to food production, is undergoing one of the most extreme transformations in its grain-producing sector of any country in the study. Ethiopia shows little change in the mix of grains produced but is one of the most food-dependent countries in the world. This is another reason why the dynamics of changes in the composition of grain production must be analyzed on a country-by-country basis.

As will be discussed in greater detail below, the patterns of substitution of grains in production vary from one country to another, but some discernible regional trends exist. In Latin America, for example, government policies and international and national research programs have combined to make grains other than maize more profitable. Sorghum and rice are the principal grains replacing maize in Latin American countries. In several sub-Saharan African countries, wheat and rice are displacing maize, sorghum, and millet. In southern Asia, wheat is supplanting rice, sorghum, and millet.

The most widespread pattern is the replacement of food grains by grains for animal feed. A number of recent studies of worldwide consumption trends have demonstrated that in developing countries as a whole, the growth of feed use of basic staples (both cereals and noncereals) is outstripping that of food use. One such study has shown that while basic food production in developing countries grew at an annual rate of 3.1% between 1961 and 1980, food consumption grew at 3.2%, and feed consumption at 4.3%. The resulting gap between production and consumption was closed by a threefold increase in net imports of basic staples to the Third World (Paulino 1986:26–31).

Another study cites a UN estimate that more than three-fourths of the coarse grains imported to developing countries were destined for feed use in 1981. (Coarse grains include all grains except wheat and rice.) The use of cereal grains and by-products for feed in developing countries increased by 4.6% per year between 1966–1970 and 1976–1980, while the growth of livestock products rose by only 3.4%, according to that report, which projected to the year 2000 an increase in cereal feed demand from 4.7% to 5.5% per year to sustain a 3.7% growth in livestock production (Sarma 1986:10).

The most accelerated rates of conversion from food to feed are occurring in Mexico and Central America, upper South America, eastern and southeastern Asia, northern Africa, and western Asia, as will be discussed further on regional and individual country bases.

The shift from food grains to feed grains has significant socioeconomic consequences. The differential impacts of these changes on social groups has further polarized many societies in the Third World. Most of the world's population cannot afford to eat meat; thus, the shift in land use primarily benefits urban middle and upper income groups. In addition to the expansion of feed grain cultivation, nontraditional higher priced grains for middle and upper income markets and for export are displacing traditional food grains. In some countries, small producers have abandoned large portions of land because food grain production is no longer profitable.

In some cases, gains in yields have offset the decline in cultivated area dedicated to food grains. In others, official programs to promote basic cereal production have counteracted market forces. But the question for each country is: How long can the scientific and technical advances ease the situation—yields cannot go up forever—and at what cost? In those countries that have adopted official support programs for food crops the question is: Do these policies represent long-term commitments or temporary adjustments to food and economic crises?

WORLD GRAIN TRADE: COMPOSITION AND GROWTH

In most countries where there has been a net loss of basic cereal land to commercial agriculture, we expected to discern two effects on trade: (1) the composition of grain imports would change; and (2) the net grain trade balance would deteriorate both in terms of increased quantity and value of grain imports relative to grain exports.

In the first instance, many countries that decreased acreage in staple food grains made up for the relative decline in production by increasing imports of that staple in comparison to other grains. This is so for Brazil, Mexico, Venezuela, South Africa, and Tanzania (maize), Morocco (wheat), and Nigeria (maize and sorghum). In these countries, the most common pattern was a dramatic rise in maize imports from the developed market economies to compensate for the relative decline in area devoted to this grain.

In other cases, countries showed a pattern of increasing imports of the grains that were also expanding in domestic production, thus indicating that even increasing supplies at home did not keep pace with domestic demand. This pattern is evident in Colombia, Mexico, and Venezuela (sorghum), Algeria (barley), Egypt, Zimbabwe, and the Philippines (maize), Nigeria and Tanzania (rice), Bangladesh (wheat), and Thailand (maize and sorghum). Sorghum, maize, and barley imports to these countries were destined primarily for feed use. Rice imports to African countries respond primarily to increased demand in middle and upper income urban markets. Imports of wheat to Bangladesh were geared toward low income urban markets.

In Table V, we summarize for each country for the period 1961–1986: (1) the grains that have increased in area cultivated relative to other grains; (2) those that have experienced a relative decline in cultivation; (3) grains that have expanded as a proportion of total grain imports; and (4) whether the value of the net grain balance has improved (+) or deteriorated (–).

The second effect, the net increase in grain imports, characterizes all but six of the developing countries reviewed here. Only Argentina, Turkey, South Africa, Zimbabwe, India, and Thailand have not experienced a net increase in grain imports. This trend holds true even if the crisis years of the early to mid-1980s are excluded. Other studies have found that this trend in increasing food dependency also holds true for all cereal and noncereal food staples. Since the 1960s, developing countries as a group have increased net imports of basic food staples threefold. Sub-Saharan Africa and Latin America have gone from net food-exporting to net importing regions (Paulino 1986:31).

Turkey is the only country that has made the transition from a net grain-importing to net grain-exporting country, primarily through dramatic changes in wheat technology. Of the six countries included in the study that were grain exporters in 1960, two have become major net importers (Mexico and Kenya). The others (Argentina, Thailand, South Africa, and Zimbabwe) have improved their status as grain-exporting countries. India is the only grain-importing country that has improved its net grain trade balance, but it is still heavily dependent on food imports.

Of the 13 countries that underwent a relative decline in the area cultivated in food grain staples, 10 experienced a major decline in their balance of grain trade. Included in this group are Brazil, Colombia, Mexico, Peru, Venezuela, Egypt, Nigeria, Sudan, Tanzania, and the Philippines. South Africa, India, and Thailand improved their net grain trade position despite the loss of land in staple food grains.

Those countries, however, that increased their cultivation of staple grains or suffered no major substitution in grain production also experienced a deterioration in their grain trade. These countries are Algeria, Morocco, Burkina Faso, Ethiopia, Kenya, Bangladesh, Indonesia, and China. The Asian countries in this list did improve their ratio of imports to exports with respect to the volume of grains traded but still suffered a major deterioration in their net grain trade balance.

The substitution of grains in production within developing countries may therefore contribute to increases in food imports, but government policies and other factors clearly influence the kind and quantity of imports. Where no substitution in grain production is occurring, natural disasters and changes in international and national commodity prices, among other factors, have contributed to the deterioration in net grain trade.

THE SUBSTITUTION OF GRAINS AS SOCIAL CHANGE

Our perspective is that the shift in agricultural production involves more than a simple substitution of one product for another. These processes are not socially or geographically neutral; they are important to document and comprehend because they are representative of profound social and political changes that are occurring in developing countries. That is, where traditional food crops are being displaced, so too are small-scale food producers.

In most developing countries small-scale producers still feed the bulk of the population. Historically, they have grown enough food to meet their own needs plus most of the basic food needs of the domestic population. As developing countries are increasingly integrated into the world economy, however, there is a growing competition between small-scale food producers and commercial growers over the use of the available agricultural resources, particularly credit and the most fertile land. Producers of staple foods for the domestic market compete unequally with growers whose production is oriented toward more profitable export commodities or more expensive domestic goods.

Decisions by these different groups of producers as to what kinds of crops to cultivate are based on substantially different criteria. Small-scale producers have tended historically to meet their own food needs first and sell surplus food in regional or national markets. In spite of the unfavorable terms on which they can participate in the market, these sales have generally allowed them to purchase the nonfood items they need for their subsistence. On the other hand, profitability is the determining criterion for commercially oriented growers. This is not to suggest that small-scale producers are not interested in earning cash profits, but rather that profitability is not the only or frequently the major consideration in decisionmaking.

Because traditional cereal staples tend to have low market prices relative to other agricultural commodities, they are usually less profitable crops. These low market values are a historical heritage. National government policies that fix low prices for staple food crops, in order to maintain low consumer costs, broaden this gap in profitability between staple food crops and export or luxury crops. Thus, with the integration of developing countries into world commodity markets, there is a tendency for the more profitable (commercial) crops to expand in acreage. Because small-scale producers often lack the resources necessary to grow commercial or export-oriented crops, they may not be able to participate in this growth. On the contrary, they may find that the commercial expansion has an inflationary impact on production costs and land rent that may even make their traditional production less feasible. Small producers may abandon their land or may be squeezed or bought out by larger commercial interests, which may expand their operations by absorbing the lands of small producers. In other cases, land suited to basic staple crops but not profitable for others may be abandoned and taken out of production altogether (see DeWalt and Barkin 1987; Barkin and DeWalt 1988).

This process may lead to a number of possible outcomes: (1) small producers may completely abandon their land, which may remain unproductive if it is suited to basic staple crops but not to commercial ones; (2) small producers who have access to the necessary resources may convert their land to commercial crops; or (3) small producers who cannot make the change may be bought out by larger commercial interests (see DeWalt 1983, 1985c, 1986). Those producers who are squeezed out may move to more marginal land, migrate to urban centers or other regions for wage work, or join the growing ranks of the unemployed. Because the change from traditional food crop production to large-scale commercial production is usually accompanied by a change from labor-intensive to more capital-intensive forms of production, we would expect this process of substitution to be accompanied by a relative decline in the agricultural labor force.

This pattern of substitution of staple foods by commercial crops and the corresponding displacement of small producers may occur in a number of different ways. In this study, we focus on grain producers and the substitution of grains in production because, as noted previously, grains constitute the bulk of world food production. Substitution may include the displacement of human food grains by: grain for processed animal feed; grain to meet the demands of urban middle and upper class consumers; grain for export to earn foreign exchange; or other commercially attractive products for national markets or export (livestock, luxury fruits and vegetables, plantation crops, etc.). The effect, in any case, is to undermine the livelihood of much of the rural population and to decrease the availability (and increase the price) of basic staples for the bulk of the population. This conversion process exacerbates the growing food and economic crises in developing market economies and will continue to do so unless effective policies are adopted to counteract this course.

Small producers and low income consumers are the hardest hit by this pattern of substitution in production. For example, low income producers and consumers alike generally cannot afford to produce or buy the new commercial food products. Small producers rarely own more than a few yard animals; low income producers and consumers generally cannot afford to purchase meat. Thus, land and resources dedicated to grain for processed feed or to livestock represents a net loss of nutritional resources available to a major sector of the population. Similarly, land dedicated to more costly grains at the expense of traditional staples (rice versus maize, for example, in parts of Latin America and Africa) benefits more wealthy urban consumers at the expense of the low income rural and urban population.

Moreover, the trend toward the substitution of staple crops by commercial agriculture in production systems has potentially serious long-term effects. Once traditional food production systems are destroyed and small producers displaced, it is extremely difficult to reverse the process. Displaced producers often leave rural areas altogether in search of other means of livelihood. This disruption and migration is wreaking havoc with the existing organization of society in many countries, while no alternative productive activities are emerging for these displaced populations.

THE REGIONAL STUDIES

The following chapters offer a detailed introduction by region to the changing pattern of grain cultivation and trade for each of the 24 developing countries in the study. In each of these chapters we examine the quantitative trends observed in each of the areas and discuss the distributional implications for producers and consumers of the global process of the substitution of grains in production. The analysis follows the country-to-country variations, while continually attempting to identify discernible regional patterns. In Latin America, for example, where maize is the common staple cereal, it is being replaced by more profitable grains—primarily sorghum, followed by rice. In several sub-Saharan African countries, wheat and rice are displacing maize, sorghum, and millet. In southern Asia, wheat is supplanting rice, sorghum, and millet. Perhaps the most important lesson to be gleaned from this work is that the variability of country-specific results makes suspect conclusions derived from the various forms of aggregation common in many analyses of the world grain situation.

3
The Substitution of Grains in Latin America

REGIONAL OVERVIEW

Of the world's developing countries, those of Latin America have undergone the most extensive process of grain substitution in production and trade. Land dedicated to maize, the common human cereal for most of the continent, is in relative decline compared to other crops. For Latin America as a whole, maize acreage has declined from 56% to 51% of the total cultivated cropland. The introduction of high yielding varieties of maize and other technological modifications during this period has somewhat lessened the impact of the relative decline in maize cultivation, but not enough to offset the need for significant increases in maize imports throughout the region.

Sorghum for animal feed is the major grain displacing maize, particularly in Argentina, Colombia, Mexico, and Venezuela. Only in Argentina does the substitution involve one feed grain for another. In Latin America as a whole over the last 25 years, sorghum acreage has increased by two and a half times, from 4% of the land area to 10%. Rice and, following it, wheat (for changing middle and upper income diets) are the other major grains replacing the cultivation of traditional staples (rice in Colombia, Peru, and Venezuela; wheat in Brazil).

In Table VI, we present this pattern of substitution of grains in production that has taken place in each Latin American country over the last 25 years. With the exception of Argentina and Brazil, the increases and decreases in cultivated area represent steady trends. In Argentina, cultivated land in maize grew from 27% of the total in 1961–1965 to 30% in 1966–1970, and then declined to 25% of the total grain area in 1981–1985. In Brazil, wheat production rose from 6% of total cultivated grain land in 1961–1965 to 16% of the total area in the period 1976–1980 before falling to 11% in the 1980s. The drop in area in the 1980s was due in part to government policies specifically adopted to support production of basic foods, which include maize, beans, and cassava. Similarly, maize cultivation for direct consumption in Brazil decreased from 62% to 54% of the area between 1961–1965 and 1976–1980 and then climbed back to 59% in the 1980s.

Following the approach to the adoption and diffusion of crops developed in agricultural sciences, we would expect that grains introduced into new regions would experience higher yields and growth rates of yields than in their traditional environment. This trend generally holds true for sorghum: The average yields and growth rates of yields of sorghum were considerably higher in Latin America as a whole compared to Africa or Asia, as indicated in Table VII (see the Appendix for a detailed comparison of data on yields). Of the 24 countries included in this study, the six Latin American countries ranked among the top seven in terms of growth in sorghum output. The growth rate of sorghum in Latin America as a whole was 3.5 times greater than the world average. By contrast, in Africa and Asia, where sorghum is a traditional food crop, the growth rates were, respectively, one-fifth and one-twentieth that of Latin America.

The data on comparative rice yields and growth rates between Latin American countries and Asian countries is less clear. The variation in the yields and growth rates of yields for rice among Asian countries, as well as among Latin American countries, is considerable. As indicated in Table VIII, there is also substantial variation between the average yields and growth rates of yields of sorghum in the Latin American countries in the study.

Moreover, while we would expect a high correlation between increasing acreage and increasing yields of nontraditional versus traditional grains (sorghum and rice versus maize in Latin America), this correlation holds in some cases, but not others. In Colombia, Mexico, and Peru, the 25-year average yields and growth rates of sorghum and rice were considerably higher than those of maize. In Argentina, however, the growth rates of sorghum yields were lower than those of maize. And in Venezuela, while the average yields of sorghum were slightly higher than those of maize, maize yields grew at 2.9% per year while those of sorghum showed no consistent upward trend. These patterns are evident from a comparison of Tables VII and VIII. Other explanations, then, are needed to comprehend the dramatic growth of sorghum and rice.

When area and yields are taken into consideration, sorghum output in Latin America has increased at two and a half times the rate of maize. Sorghum has outpaced maize in both the growth in yields and increase in cultivated area. Surprisingly, however, sorghum expansion in Latin America has occurred much more as a result of increases in cultivated area than in yield. By contrast, the growth in overall maize production, at a rate slightly less than the world average of 3.6% per year, has been due primarily to yield increases. Nevertheless, the growth in maize yields was not sufficient to offset the decline in production caused by the sharp drop in cultivated land in maize.

To summarize, the data on area, yields, and production of grains in the Latin American countries reviewed here chronicle a major transformation in agriculture away from the cultivation of traditional staple cereals for direct consumption toward the production of nontraditional and commercially profitable commodities. The displacement of maize by sorghum, rice, and wheat represents a shift from foods produced and consumed by small-scale farmers and low income consumers to those oriented toward middle and upper income markets. These patterns of displacement of maize by sorghum, rice, and wheat cannot be explained by agronomic factors alone but must be understood in the context of changing socioeconomic conditions in Latin American countries.

Soaring imports of maize have accompanied the relative loss of cultivated maize area from 1961 to 1985. Taken as a whole, imports of maize to Latin America grew at an annual rate of 11.7%, climbing from 7% of total grain imports in 1961–1965 to 44% in 1981–1985. In South America (excluding Central America and the Caribbean) maize imports grew at an average of 15.7% per year. Of the countries in our study, maize imports are rising relative to other grains in every country but Colombia (see Table IX). In addition, in three of the six countries—Colombia, Mexico, and Venezuela—the increase in sorghum production has not kept pace with domestic demand, thus requiring major imports of sorghum as well as maize.

While the significant decline in maize production in Latin American countries explains the need for increased maize imports, the rise in sorghum imports is more unexpected. Despite the massive expansion of sorghum production destined for animal feed, major increases of imports to Colombia, Mexico, and Venezuela have occurred. This increased demand is largely the result of the growing percentage of grains destined for livestock, promoted through the establishment of local subsidiaries of the international feed companies that has fed the growth of the livestock industry since the 1960s (see Reig 1980; Arroyo *et al.* 1980; Suárez and Vigorito 1981/2; Suárez and Rodríguez 1984; Vigorito 1984).

All of the countries reviewed here, except Argentina, have suffered a major deterioration of their net grain trade balance (see Table X). The Mexican case is the most noteworthy: A major exporter of grains by the late 1960s as a result of land reform measures and investments in irrigation, coupled with a successful green revolution in wheat, the country is now one of the region's top grain importers—primarily of maize and sorghum.

Although the high yields of sorghum encourage adoption and rapid diffusion of its cultivation, the surge in the domestic demand for sorghum for livestock feed owes more to the expansion of livestock production and changes in the industry's technology throughout Latin America during the last 30 years. Between 1950 and 1980, livestock production grew at a faster rate than did overall crop production in Brazil, Mexico, Peru, and Venezuela. In Brazil and Mexico, for example, livestock increased its share of total agricultural output from 24% to 38% and from 28% to 42% respectively. In Colombia, both sectors grew at equal rates (Elias 1985:19).

The industrialization of livestock production throughout the continent further increased demand for animal feed. Cattle, once raised on natural pastures, and pigs and chickens, formerly fed on the wastes of farms, are now fattened with animal feeds. Sorghum constitutes approximately 75% of those feeds (DeWalt 1985a:43).

There are agronomic, economic, and social reasons, however, why sorghum in particular has come to form the base of animal feed, and why it has displaced maize so rapidly and extensively. First, sorghum is more drought tolerant than is maize and was initially experimented with to resolve problems of production in marginal areas where rainfall was limited or unevenly distributed (Pitner *et al.* 1954:1). Second, sorghum is of the same family of grasses as maize, and agronomists thought it would be relatively easy for maize farmers to convert to sorghum production: "The cultivation of sorghums is so nearly like that of corn that sorghums can readily be grown by farmers already accustomed to handling corn" (Rockefeller Foundation 1957:77). With the growth in demand for industrial feed, sorghum became much more commercially profitable than was maize because in many countries, such as Mexico, governments have maintained maize at prices below world market levels and real production costs.

Additionally, sorghum cultivation is highly mechanized and therefore benefits from government policies aimed at modernizing agriculture through subsidies and/or credits for tractors, improved seeds, fertilizers, and other inputs. Individual producers, small- and large-scale alike, also see benefits in planting sorghum, which is much less labor-intensive than is maize. Maize requires two to ten times more person-days of labor per hectare, primarily because harvest practices make it more difficult to mechanize (Barkin and DeWalt 1988). As a result of its drought tolerance, sorghum is also a much less risky plant to cultivate. These and other factors have combined to make sorghum the growth crop throughout the region.

COUNTRY ANALYSES

Colombia

Colombia historically has been relatively self-sufficient in food production. During the period 1961 through 1986, the 3.2% annual growth rate of cereal production outpaced population growth of 2.4%. The average growth in per capita cereal supply, taking into account production and trade, was 1.4%.

Per capita statistics, however, are misleading. A number of studies have documented that malnutrition is a serious, and perhaps growing, problem in Colombia. Although per capita availability of calories is above the minimum dietary recommendations of the FAO, food consumption is highly uneven between income groups and between urban and rural areas. Poverty limits consumption; the 50% of population that earns less than 20% of national income spends 60% of its income on food. Five percent of the population earns 33% of the national income, according to a recent U.S. Department of Agriculture

(USDA) study. As a result, "malnutrition is a widespread phenomenon in Colombia." Twenty percent of the Colombian population consumes 40% of the minimum dietary recommendations while half of the population consumes less than 70% of the minimum requirements (Bolling 1987:14; García García 1981:126–137).

Colombia's primary staple grain is maize; cassava, potatoes, and plantains also serve as significant food crops. Domestically produced and imported wheat and rice figure prominently in middle and upper income diets. For the population as a whole, 30% of the average caloric intake comes from cereals, and another 10% from roots and tubers. Dependence on cereals, roots, and tubers is much greater for lower income people (Bolling 1987).[2]

In the past 25 years, Colombian agriculture has shifted away from domestic food production and self-sufficiency. Between 1961–1965 and 1981–1985, overall grain imports to Colombia quadrupled in volume and equaled 25% of domestic grain production, up from 11.6% in the early 1960s. While wheat continued to constitute the bulk of the imports, its share declined from 88% of the total in 1961–1965 to 70% in 1981–1985; imports of sorghum and barley (both feed grains) grew from zero in 1961–1965 to 9% and 13% respectively of total grain imports in 1981–1985 (see Table IX). Although the volume of maize imports also increased, its share of the total remained small, growing from 5.3% to 7.6% in the 25-year period.

This increase in food dependency has occurred in part in response to government policies since the 1960s, promoting certain agricultural commodities for export, including rice, coffee, cotton, and sugar. Beginning in the late 1960s, the government introduced a number of reforms to encourage export production, including a series of currency devaluations (currency was considered overvalued and favored imports), fiscal incentives for exports, a new export promotion fund, free trade zones, and the Andean Pact with a common external tariff (Helmsing 1986:151).[3]

At the same time, the Colombian government adopted policies to stimulate agricultural productivity of export-oriented commodities through the use of new technological innovations, including new high yielding varieties, chemical inputs, mechanization of production, and irrigation. The growth of large-scale agriculture and a more highly capitalized production yields exportable surpluses in cotton, sugar, and rice. Growing agricultural exports included coffee (which grew from 43% of total export earnings in 1974 to 65% in 1986), as well as cocoa, palm oil, and nontraditional exports such as rice, sugar, and cotton (Helmsing 1986:150–156).

As a result, export crops expanded in area, while cereal cultivation as a proportion of overall harvested area declined significantly in this period—from 39% of the total area in 1961–1965 to 31.7% in 1976–1980. An absolute reduction in the area cultivated in maize, and secondarily wheat, accounted for this overall decline in cereal cultivation (Bolling 1987).

Small-scale producers are the primary suppliers of maize, roots, tubers, and wheat. The first three crops are grown for home consumption and sale in regional and national markets, while wheat serves primarily as a cash crop. In Cundinamarca, for example, one of the nation's major wheat-producing states, nearly 40% of the wheat is grown on farms of less than 10 hectares, of which only 1 hectare is planted in wheat (Hall 1985:144).

By contrast, rice, which requires more agricultural inputs and irrigation, tends to be grown by large-scale producers. Official government policy in Colombia seeks to integrate food policy with agricultural production policy through the maintenance of support prices and the regulation of supplies of food crops. These include sorghum, soybeans, potatoes, sesame, barley, rice, maize, wheat, and beans. While this policy may prevent serious losses during disaster years, it has not ensured the maintenance of prior levels of production of basic food crops such as maize, wheat, beans, and potatoes (Hall 1985:143).

Within the grain-producing sector, commercial sorghum and rice growers have displaced maize and wheat producers. Sorghum acreage grew from 1% of the total cereal land in 1961–1965 to 19% in 1981–1985. Rice increased from 24% to 31% of the cereal land in the same period. By contrast, maize declined from 61% of the land in grains to 45% in the last 25 years; wheat currently covers only 3% of the area, down from 10% in 1961–1965 (see Table VI). This transformation affects over 25% of the land in cereal production, second only to Venezuela in terms of the magnitude of this change. Table XI presents a comparison of the average area, yields, and production of these grains for the 25-year period and their average annual growth rates.

Government policies also effectively discouraged wheat cultivation. The Agricultural Marketing Institute (IDEMA), the sole purchaser and distributor of wheat, obtained supplies from the U.S. food aid program until the mid-1970s. These concessionary purchases of wheat under PL 480 allowed the Colombian government to sell imported wheat at relatively low prices, thus discouraging domestic production. By 1971–1975, the area in wheat cultivation was only 40% of what it had been in 1961–1965. As a result, wheat imports, already high, grew even more substantially in the 1970s and 1980s.

During this same period, Colombian wheat farms were relatively undeveloped in technological and commercial terms; the small-scale producers were unorganized and thus not in a position to influence government price policy. By contrast, large-scale rice growers were organized into the National Federation of Rice Growers (FEDEARROZ), which succeeded in obtaining government restrictions on rice imports, lower duties on imported fertilizers and machinery, and better credit conditions and price supports. As a result, rice cultivation grew relative to that of wheat. While rice grew from 24% to 31% of the total grain area, wheat cultivation decreased by the same percentage (from 10% to 3% of the total). IDEMA used the revenues from PL 480 wheat sales to increase support prices for rice growers (Hall 1985).

With a domestic price slightly higher than that for wheat and 30% higher than that for maize during the 1970s, rice is primarily a middle and upper income food item (Bolling 1987:16). It is also a growing export commodity. While Colombian grain exports have remained relatively small, they are made up entirely of rice.

In summary, then, the process of the substitution of grains in production in Colombia—of rice for maize and wheat—appears to have had significant impacts on producers and consumers alike. On the one hand, it has been accompanied by a displacement of small-scale maize and wheat producers by large-scale rice growers. Smallholder peasant agriculture has been marginalized, and agricultural employment (which had increased in the 1950s) has dropped substantially. The number of smallholdings (those less than 5 hectares), for example, declined from 756,000 in 1960 to 640,000 in 1970 (Helmsing 1986:150–157). For consumers, on the other hand, retail prices for all food grains rose dramatically during the 1970s, but prices of maize rose faster than did those of rice and wheat.[4]

Thus, from the perspective of producer and consumer welfare, as well as that of national food self-sufficiency, the transformations in Colombian agriculture in the last 25 years do not appear to have moved the country or the bulk of its population toward increased prosperity, but rather toward an increased polarization between those who benefit from the transformations in agriculture and those who do not.

Mexico

Mexico's "agricultural miracle" from the 1940s to 1965—an annual growth rate of 5.7% in agricultural production—led it to achieve food self-sufficiency by the 1960s (Yates 1981; Carmona *et al.* 1983).[5] Food self-sufficiency was achieved through a combination of factors: extensive land reform that gave small producers access to land along with increased credit; government-sponsored irrigation projects to increase food cultivation, which resulted in the expansion of irrigated land from less than 14% in 1950 to 22% by the mid-1970s; and the introduction of high yielding varieties of seeds, particularly wheat, accompanied by the increased use of fertilizers, tractors, and other inputs.

Mexico's growth rate of 4.6% in cereal production between 1961–1965 and 1981–1985 continued to surpass its population growth of 3% during the same period. But by the mid-1970s, Mexico was a net importer of food. Maize and wheat imports grew at an annual rate of 11.5% and 12.6% between 1961–1965 and 1981–1985, but particularly jumped after 1970 (the volume of grain imports was 10 times higher in 1971–1975 than in 1966–1970).

The phenomenal expansion of sorghum, Mexico's "second green revolution" (DeWalt 1985a), provides an important part of the explanation for the country's return to food dependency. Sorghum production grew in response to the dramatic growth and industrialization of livestock production during this period. Sorghum became the main ingredient in industrialized feed. Between 1950 and 1975, the number of establishments producing animal feed grew from 19 to over 305, and since then the number has been growing explosively.

Thus, Mexico's growth in cereal production during this time is largely accounted for by sorghum output. Sorghum covered 2% of the grain land in 1961–1965 and 16% in 1981–1985; maize suffered a corresponding drop from 83% to 69% of the cultivated area (see Table VI). The production of beans, an important staple food traditionally intercropped with maize, has declined at approximately the same rate as that of maize.

Despite the extraordinary growth in sorghum cultivation, the share of cereal in overall harvested area actually declined between 1961 and 1986. Cereals made up 62.6% of the total cropland in 1961–1965 and 52.2% in 1981–1985. Similarly, maize dropped from 51.6% of the total to 36.6%, while sorghum increased its share from 1.5% to 8%. Thus, in addition to the substitution of sorghum for maize in grain production, there was a major substitution of export-oriented crops for cereals as a whole. These export crops, primarily destined for the U.S. market, included fruits and vegetables (e.g., tomatoes, melons, oranges, strawberries).[6]

Moreover, sorghum yields have been much higher than those of maize and approach those of wheat (see Table VIII). In contrast to maize, sorghum production in Mexico has become primarily a large-scale, capital-intensive, and highly mechanized operation. Sorghum producers have taken advantage of government credits for tractors, fertilizers, and other inputs to modernize their operations. Virtually all sorghum in Mexico is grown from hybrid seed, supplied by transnational seed companies such as DeKalb, Pioneer, Northrup-King, Asgrow, and Funk. Nearly one-third of all production is taking place on irrigated land, despite the fact that sorghum was originally introduced to Mexico in the 1940s to make use of marginal drylands. Sorghum expansion was highly concentrated regionally in the most productive agricultural area of Mexico, on lands formerly planted in maize and, in some cases, wheat (DeWalt 1985a; DeWalt and Barkin 1987).

The impact of the substitution of grains in production on Mexican producers, in this case with sorghum as the primary crop, has been profound. National employment figures, for example, show that while employment in the modern rural sector (i.e., commercial agriculture) expanded from 31.7% of the total employed in agriculture in 1950 to 51% in 1980, there was an absolute reduction in the number of self-employed agricultural workers (Couriel 1984:56). In other words, the rise of commercial agriculture has led to a consolidation of production into larger enterprises and a displacement of producers from their land. Case studies of Mexican agrarian reform lands have analyzed this process in greater detail (DeWalt and Barkin 1987; DeWalt et al. 1987). The inability of the economy to absorb the growing number of displaced producers has imposed additional hardships on them and has fueled the temporary and permanent migration of laborers within Mexico and to the United States.

On the other hand, low income consumers do not share in the benefits of a higher quality protein diet, available as a result of the growth in livestock and livestock-oriented cultivation, because they cannot afford to purchase meat. In 1980, for example, the Mexican government reported that over 35% of the population never eats meat (Redclift 1981:13–14). While many poor people may eat eggs and milk, the overwhelming proportion of livestock products are consumed by middle and upper income groups. As a result, malnutrition is widespread. Over 27% of the population consume less than the minimum required caloric and protein intake, according to a survey by the National Nutrition Institute (Redclift 1981). More recent studies estimate that more than one-half of the population is malnourished (Centro de Ecodesarrollo and Fundación Friedrich Naumann 1988).

Thus, despite the more than doubling of cereal production during the last 25 years, grain imports in 1981–1985 were 25 times their volume in 1961–1965 and continue to grow. Grain imports as a percentage of domestic production rose from 2.6% in 1961–1965 to 25.7% in the 1980s. See Table XII for a comparison of the average area, yields, and production of these grains for the 25-year period and the average annual growth rates.

Venezuela

Unlike Mexico and Colombia, Venezuela has not historically been a major grain-producing country nor has it been even close to self-sufficient in food. The origins of food dependency date to the turn of the century; and the reliance on food imports increased rapidly with the development of the oil industry from the 1920s. By the 1950s, oil accounted for 94% of export revenues. The urban middle and upper classes had substituted the traditional maize-based diet for international foods imported from Europe and the United States. Wheat had replaced maize as the staple grain for upper income groups (Witte Wright 1985:152).

The bulk of the population, however, still depends on multicrop systems of food production—including maize, black beans, squash, manioc, and potatoes—on small plots of land called *minifundios*. A highly skewed pattern of land distribution, however, meant that food production was relegated to a very small portion of cultivatable land while cattle, coffee, and cacao were grown on large estates. According to one estimate, in the 1950s almost two-thirds of the peasant population cultivated food crops but worked on only 3% of the land (Witte Wright 1985:153).

The Venezuelan food system began to be increasingly integrated into international markets in the 1940s, following two trade agreements with the United States in 1939 and 1941 that opened up trade in wheat by substantially reducing the heavy tariffs on wheat imports in effect until that time (Jaffé Carbonell and Rothman 1977:312). In the 1950s, with the encouragement of import-substituting policies, U.S. milling and feed corporations, including International Milling, General Mills, Pillsbury, and Ralston Purina, established subsidiaries in Venezuela. And in 1959, although it had come to power on a platform of social and economic reform, the Acción Democrática party continued the import-substituting policies of the prior regime. The development of the food industry under the aegis of U.S. corporations was viewed as a means to establish stable supplies of cheap food staples as well as to develop a market for the expansion of domestic agriculture (Witte Wright 1985).

The milling and feed industries, however, preferred imported grains, particularly U.S. wheat, and succeeded throughout most of the 1960s and 1970s in gaining special exchange rates for wheat and exemptions from import duties (Jaffé Carbonell and Rothman 1977:313). These arrangements, coupled with the availability of concessionally priced wheat under U.S. PL 480, meant that grain imports to Venezuela skyrocketed. Grain imports averaged 80% of domestic cereal production in Venezuela in 1961–1965, and wheat composed almost 90% of those imports. Total grain imports rose to 174% of domestic production by 1981–1985. By comparison, Mexican grain imports equaled 2.6% of production in 1961–1965, and climbed to 25.7% in 1981–1985. The comparable figures for Colombia are 12% in the first period and 25% in the second.

Foreign domination and concentration in the agrofood industry increased rapidly. By the mid-1970s, International Multifoods and General Mills processed more than 50% of imported wheat; in the animal feed industry, Ralston Purina, International Foods-Monaca, Polar, and the Mendoza-Boulton group (the largest national firm) controlled 85% of production; and in poultry production, Ralston Purina, General Mills, and E. Mendoza accounted for 60% of output (Teubal 1987:344).

The domestic agricultural sector, in the meantime, was left to stagnate. Government policies favored large-scale enterprises that were modernizing production. The early promises of land reform of the Acción Democrática failed to materialize. An effort by the Ministry of Agriculture to improve maize production (El Plan de Maíz) was discarded after a year of operation, despite apparent increases in production in response to the program. And agriculture received less than 10% of the budget for most years (Witte Wright 1985:160–162). Grain production in Venezuela equaled only 8% of the value of agricultural output (González B. 1986:16).

Government policies such as these encouraged a shift in land utilization: The share of maize in cereal land and overall cultivated land consistently declined, particularly between 1960 and 1985. It represented an estimated 95% of cereal cultivation in the 1930s, averaged 84% of grain cultivation in 1961–1965 but dropped to 45% by 1981–1985—the largest percentage decline of any Latin American country in this study (see Table VI).

The substitution of grains in production in Venezuela involved the displacement of maize by sorghum and rice. The first decline in maize cultivation was due to efforts to diversify grain production in the 1940s and 1950s that led to the expansion of rice cultivation, geared primarily to the middle and upper income markets. Rice grew to cover 15% of cereal land by 1961–1965. It expanded to 25% of the land by 1981–1985. The expansion in cultivated acreage was significant (3.6% per year), and yields, already almost double those of maize, grew additionally at 2.4% annually during the period 1961–1985. Thus, the growth in rice production of 6% per year was more than double that of maize at 2.7% (see Table XIII). An analysis of the costs of production versus producer prices for rice and maize shows that rice is almost 2.5 times more profitable than is maize, even though the producer prices for maize have been consistently rising and, for the first time, surpassed those of rice in 1984 (González B. 1986:26).

The more dramatic transformation in agriculture came with the takeoff of sorghum in the mid-1970s. Beginning in 1968, Ralston Purina and Protinal (the largest national feed corporation, owned by the Mendoza family) assisted the Ministry of Agriculture and the University of Zula in the introduction and development of commercial sorghum production (Witte Wright 1985:158). Although sorghum averaged only 2.8% of the land in cereal cultivation in 1971–1975, by the 1976–1980 period, it covered 23.3% of the land, increasing to 29.8% in the 1980s. While sorghum acreage expanded at 27% annually, yields showed no consistent increases. Average sorghum yields in Venezuela of 1.6 kg/ha are considerably behind those of Mexico (2.9), Colombia (2.3), and Argentina (2.3). The dramatic expansion in acreage, however, at the expense of maize production, compensates for the low yields. And despite the extraordinary growth of commercial production, sorghum imports have increased from zero to over 600,000 tons per year, currently representing 23% of grain imports.

Commercial production of both sorghum and rice, then, accounts for significant increases in grain output during this period, while maize production has stagnated. Total grain production has grown at 5.2% annually, the highest of the six Latin American countries in this study. Its rate of expansion of cereal area equals that of Brazil (2.5% per year), and cereals actually increased as a proportion of total cultivated area, from 35.8% in 1961–1965 to 40% in 1976–1980. We set out in Table XIII the significant changes that have occurred in the grain sector during the past 25 years.

Despite these gains in output, however, Venezuela's grain imports have risen fivefold in the last 25 years. The composition of imports has also changed: Wheat, which constituted 88% of imports in 1961–1965, now equals 35%. Maize imports, making up for declining production, have grown from 9% to 41.8%; and, as in Mexico, despite the dramatic surge in domestic production of sorghum, it does not satisfy domestic demand.

Some researchers argue that the major reason for Venezuela's expansion of imports is that domestic grain prices far exceed international prices, making domestic grains uncompetitive. In 1981, the price of domestic maize was double the international price, and the gap has increased since then. Rice, the grain that is closest to the international price, is still 30% higher (González B. 1986:27–28). But such price policies are part of a constellation of government and private efforts that have favored the growth and concentration of a food industry dominated by a handful of national and international companies at the expense of small-scale food producers. This strategy failed to reduce the price of staple foods. Instead, Venezuela experienced serious food price inflation in the 1970s, and the country dramatically increased its dependency on food imports. In the meantime, the food industry concentrated on developing new luxury and packaged foods as well as meat products that low income people cannot afford. As a result, the incidence of malnutrition has changed little: The number of deaths caused by malnutrition in 1974 was the same as it had been in 1950. And the proportion of school-age children with height and weight deficiencies has increased since 1960 (Witte Wright 1985:166).

Argentina

Argentina differs significantly from the other Latin American countries included in our study. First, it has historically been a large grain exporting country, and substantially improved its net grain trade balance during the 25-year period reviewed here. Second, although Argentina has undergone major substitutions in grain production since 1960, these changes primarily involved the substitution of one feed grain for another.

Up until the Great Depression, in 1929, Argentina's development strategy was based on the expansion of food production for national markets and for export, particularly to England. Blessed with substantial agricultural resources, the economy grew rapidly, and Argentina appeared to be a "developed" country in many ways. The failures of the populist government of Perón (1946–1955) and of the strategy of import substitution industrialization have resulted in the familiar patterns of large foreign debt, high inflation rates, and a substantial segment of the population suffering from inadequate nutrition.

In this context, Argentina's grain exporting sector has remained successful. Between 1961–1965 and 1981–1985, the volume of grain exports increased from 6.8 to 18.5 million metric tons, a rate of 5.4% per year; grain imports decreased at an annual rate of 7.7% per annum. During the same period, the value of net grain trade grew eightfold, to an average of U.S. $2.4 million between 1981 and 1985 (Table X). Other studies have noted the importance of this growth in grain exports to offset the decline in the country's traditionally large beef exports, a decline caused by dwindling world markets (Interamerican Development Bank 1986:75, 110). Nonetheless, the value of grain exports as a percentage of total agricultural exports has fallen from 62% to 53% during the 25-year period we consider.

Significantly, the composition of grain exports has also shifted from a reliance on higher priced wheat and maize to lower priced sorghum: wheat and maize, which respectively comprised 44% and 42% of the total volume of grain exports in 1961–1965, represented 37% each of grain exports in 1981–1985. Barley and oats fell from 3% and 5% of grain exports, respectively, to virtually zero in the same period. By contrast, the share of sorghum in total grain exports grew from 7% to 26%. In value terms, the share of wheat fell from 48% to 42% and that of maize from 38% to 35%, while sorghum rose from 5% to 20% of the value of total grain exports.

These changes in the composition of grain exports reflect the pattern of substitution of grains in production during the same period. The share of land cultivated in sorghum grew from 8% to 18% between 1961–1965 and 1981–1985, while that of maize fell relatively from 30% in 1966–1970 to 25% in 1981–1985. Land devoted to barley, rye, and oats declined in absolute terms and in relative terms, from 5% to less than 3% of cultivated land (see Table VI).

The data on wheat acreage and output show a somewhat mixed picture. For the 1961–1965 to 1971–1975 period, the share of land in wheat cultivation declined substantially, from 47% to 38% of total grain land. Low yields and yield increases meant that wheat output fell from 49% to 31% of total grain output. The share of wheat in total grain exports also declined from 42% to 23% during the same period. Sorghum, and to a lesser extent maize, supplanted wheat exports. At the same time, Argentina imported wheat between 1965 and 1975. Although grain imports were only a fraction of exports, wheat constituted between 35% and 40% of those imports during this period. Beginning in the 1976–1980 period, the share of wheat in grain cultivation began to rise, reaching 50% of total grain land by the 1981–1985 period. Despite the recovery of wheat acreage, however, low wheat yields and yield growth rates relative to sorghum and maize meant that wheat constituted only 38% of total grain output in the latter period (Table XIV).

Unlike in Colombia, Mexico, and Venezuela, these shifts in land use in Argentina do not appear to have had much effect on food self-sufficiency. Sorghum is supplanting crops — maize, oats, barley, and rye — that were grown primarily for feed, fodder, or other industrial uses (e.g., beer-making). Nevertheless, we need much more information on why these changes in agricultural production occurred, and the impact of these changes on producers and consumers is deserving of further empirical research. Regional and local-level case studies are needed to assess the differential social impacts of these changing patterns of agricultural production in relation to government policies affecting the agricultural sector.

Brazil

The transformation of agriculture in Brazil shares some overall similarities with that in Mexico, Colombia, and Venezuela. Brazil enjoyed a dramatic growth of nonfood crops and export commodities at the expense of domestic staple food production; the modernization of production of nonfood crops; the increased concentration of land in commercial agroenterprises; the consequent increase in urban migration and a large unemployed work force; and the continued rise in food imports and food prices. The specifics of the Brazilian case, however, are unique.

Historically, basic food crop production in Brazil has been of secondary importance in the agricultural sector—secondary to export-oriented plantations producing coffee, cotton, and sugarcane, and extensive cattle latifundios. With respect to food production for the internal market:

> Some took place on the poorest lands of the large farms to provide food for the workers (or slaves); some was undertaken by free workers living on lands lying between the latifundios (where an important labor reserve for the large landlords was concentrated), a mass of population obliged to supplement their income by working for the landlords, because of the insufficient plot of land (minifundio) allowed them; finally, food production took place on the ever-expanding agricultural frontier (Romeiro 1987:79).

As a result, Brazil has experienced ongoing food supply problems and import dependency since colonial times.

Cassava, beans, rice, and maize are the traditional staple foods of Brazil.[7] As is evident from Table XV, cassava and beans compose a much greater percentage of low income and rural diets, decreasing in importance with increased income and urbanization. In rural areas, these foods constitute 58.5% of the caloric intake of the poorest 15% of the population and 53.2% for the lowest thirtieth percentile. Even among low income urban dwellers, and the middle and upper income rural population, however, these two traditional staples make up approximately one-quarter of the total caloric intake. Maize and rice contribute an additional 15% and 20%, respectively, of the calories of the lowest income rural and urban groups. These two staple grains increase in importance for the higher income groups.

These food staples, basic to all Brazilians, are still relegated to the leftover lands of large estates, to the *minifundios* surrounding those estates, to land abandoned after overproduction of nutrient-depleting export crops such as coffee and cotton, and to the agricultural frontier where transportation costs are great.

The most dramatic changes in the agricultural sector in recent decades have been the extraordinary rise in industrial and nontraditional export crops and a corresponding decline in the cultivation of basic food staples. This transformation is primarily due to the dramatic expansion of soybean production, beginning in the 1960s and taking off in the 1970s, and largely financed by, and exported to, Japan; and to the surge in sugarcane production for the import-substituting alcohol program initiated by the Brazilian government following the 1973 oil crisis. In Table XVI, we provide a comparison of annual growth rates of the major nonfood and food crops in the country for 1960–1970 and 1970–1980.[8]

It is significant that in the 1960s, domestic food crops were expanding in area, primarily to fill a vacuum caused by a decline in coffee production in the rich agricultural states of the south and southeast. Coffee had dominated the agricultural exports of the 1950s and had overexpanded in response to favorable world prices in the late 1950s. It had grown in production at an average rate of 12.8% (1950–1960); but a government eradication program designed to decrease acreage and increase yields led to the contraction in coffee acreage by 9.1% in the 1960s and 3.1% in the 1980s (Graham *et al.* 1987:4).

Although food crops filled this vacuum, wheat absorbed a substantial portion of the area, increasing at 6.9% per year between 1960 and 1970. Maize, beans, and cassava also experienced healthy growth rates, varying from 3.9% to 4.3% in area and 3.5% to 5.5% in output. Rice acreage and production, which had expanded more than 4% per year in the 1950s, continued to expand at that rate in area, but declining yields lowered the rice production growth rate to 2.8% between 1960 and 1970 (Graham *et al.* 1987). Government policies, however, did little to encourage growth of these crops. They lacked price supports enjoyed by commercial crops. Maize and rice prices, for example, dropped by one-third between 1955–1960 and 1965–1970 (Hall 1985:141). Thus, despite considerable growth of food crops in the 1960s, four out of the five top export crops had growth rates exceeding those of the five basic food crops, as indicated in Table XVI.

Wheat, produced commercially for growing urban markets, expanded more rapidly than did other food crops, its growth spurred by favorable government price policies established in response to a strong wheat farmers association (FECOTRIGO). Nominal wheat support prices increased tenfold between 1964 and 1970. The Brazilian government also controlled the marketing and processing of imported and domestic wheat through the office of the National Wheat Commission (CITRIN). It established a policy of buying imported wheat at a price less than that of domestic wheat and selling both domestic and imported wheat to millers for less than the price paid for domestic wheat, but more than that paid for imports. The difference between the purchase and sale prices of imported wheat helped subsidize the higher price paid for domestic wheat (Hall 1985:137).

The government then used the concessional prices of imported wheat under the U.S. PL 480 program to increase its subsidies to domestic producers. The per unit price of wheat imports declined as the quantity of imports rose. An increase of 1,000 metric tons of imported PL 480 wheat translated into an increase in wheat support prices of 100 cruzeiros per metric ton (Hall 1985:140).

The expansion of wheat also facilitated the growth of soybean production. Wheat may be intercropped with soybeans as a winter crop, and both are produced by the same large-scale mechanized operations. Soybeans, a nontraditional export crop for Brazil, grew at an annual rate of 17% in the 1960s and continued growing at 18.6% in the 1970s; this ensured that the recently converted food cropland was returned to export production.

This shift in cultivation occurred primarily in the southern and southeastern regions. Acreage in the major soybean-producing states of Paraná and Rio Grande do Sul, for example, expanded elevenfold between 1967 and 1979—from 577,000 hectares to 6,450,000 hectares. In the southern and southeastern regions, food crops dropped from 62% to 55% of the total cultivated land during the same interval (Romeiro 1987:90). Much of this expansion was financed by, and the yield exported to, Japan (San Martin and Pelegrini 1984).

Soybeans, however, also supplanted food crops in the central west, especially in the state of Mato Grosso, and in the Amazon. Nationally, domestic food production covered 67.7% of the cropland in 1970 and 59.2% in 1980; export and industrial crops rose from 32.4% to 40% of the land in the same period. Oranges and sugarcane were the two other growth crops, doubling their output growth rates between the 1960s and 1970s. The Brazilian National Alcohol Program (PROALCOOL), which officially began in 1975, was expanded in 1979 following the second oil crisis. The purpose of the program was to reduce somewhat Brazil's 80% dependence on foreign oil. The production of ethanol from sugarcane increased sevenfold by 1980—from 579 million liters to 4,000 million. Cane grown for the alcohol program has particularly expanded in the southern states of São Paulo and Paraná, and in the northern coastal states. Although a large portion of the expansion in cane occurred on grazing lands in western São Paulo, a significant amount of cropland in that state was also converted, including an estimated 338,000 hectares of maize and rice acreage between 1974 and 1979 alone. By 1980, two cassava-based distilleries were also in operation in the southeastern state of Minas Gerais, with the expectation that cassava would eventually provide the raw material for 5% of production, the total of which was projected to reach 14 billion liters by 1987 (Gray 1982:44–46).[9]

Production of sugarcane for ethanol continued to increase in the 1977–1984 period, registering an annual per capita growth rate of 7.8%; during the same period, the comparable growth rate for food crops was –1.9% and that of export crops was 2.6%. The government largely met its 10.6 billion liter production goal for 1985/86, at an estimated cost of production of U.S. $79–91 per barrel (Homem de Melo 1987:53, 57). The program has continued despite research that has documented its lack of cost effectiveness, both in terms of the enormous subsidies still required and the opportunity costs of the land and financing no longer available for export and food crops (Barzelay and Pearson 1982).

These transformations in agricultural production contributed to heightened disparities between rich and poor. An analysis of income distribution in Brazil found that between the census of 1970 and that of 1980, "inequality within the agricultural sector soared" (Denslow and Tyler 1984:1023). This finding differs from the 1960–1970 census comparisons, which indicated that inequality in overall income distribution was declining somewhat. Regional disparities also increased, between the export-oriented states in the south and southeast and the food-producing areas of the north, northeast, and central west (Graham *et al.* 1987:12).

The Brazilian government, since the mid-1960s, has played a key role in the rapid growth of modernized agriculture, the basis for the expansion of nonfood and export crops and the relative stagnation of food crops. Major allotments of subsidized credit became available beginning in the 1960s, but they were tied to the purchase of machinery, fertilizers, chemicals, and other modern inputs. The government facilitated the availability of these inputs through direct government distribution, tax exemptions, and exchange rate controls. Public expenditures improved marketing and transportation facilities and encouraged exports through rebates and tax reductions. A series of minidevaluations put the cruzeiro more in line with foreign currencies and reduced the implicit tax on agriculture (Fox 1979).[10]

Because of the high concentration of land ownership in Brazil, however, only a small portion of Brazilian farmers have been able to take advantage of these modernization policies, and most of those were concentrated in the southern and southeastern parts of the country. In 1960, land concentration was more pronounced than in 1920, and became more so, in part as a consequence of the modernization policies that favored the wealthiest producers. In 1970, 10% of the largest properties covered 77.6% of the land, while 50% of the smallest properties held 2.9%. (In 1920, the comparable areas held were 76% and 3.9%, respectively.) In 1970, 5% of the largest properties held 66.8% of the land; 1% controlled 42.8%. Moreover, much of the land was held in speculation and used as a protection against inflation. Of the estates over 10,000 hectares in size, 41.5% had a production value of less than 3,000 cruzeiros per year; 21% of the total were unexploited altogether. Land concentration and speculation continued to increase in the 1970s: In the largest grain-producing state, Paraná, for example, the number of agricultural enterprises participating in production decreased from 18% to 13% between 1972 and 1978, while the number of unexploited latifundios rose from 58% to 64% (Romeiro

1987:81–93).

Loan concentration was also extreme. Graham *et al.* (1987:24), analyzing the distribution of formal loans in relation to the percentage of producers who had access to such loans in the first place, estimated that no more than 3–4% of agricultural producers received formal credit in the 1970s.

In the process of the modernization of agriculture, land concentration increased, as small producers who were unable to compete financially lost their farms. In addition, as a result of reform legislation in the 1960s, which increased the cost of resident labor, and of the growth of mechanized agriculture (particularly in wheat and soybeans), growers found it more economical to hire seasonal migrant workers.[11] They forced small producers and tenant laborers off their estates; the displaced families moved to urban zones where the population grew from 45% to 68% of the total between 1960 and 1980. The agricultural work force dropped from 60% in 1950 to 30% in 1980, but other sectors have been unable to absorb the excess labor.

The government's export-oriented policies contributed to a doubling of cereal imports between 1961–1965 and 1981–1985, from 2.2 million tons to 5 million tons. Wheat still dominated imports, composing 88% of the total, but down from 98% of the 1961–1965 total. Notably, maize increased to 14% of grain imports in 1976–1980, but this has dropped to 6% in the 1980s. Rice rose from zero to 4% of imports in the 25-year period.

But imports of maize and rice did little to offset the decline in basic food production, or the negative impact of nutritional levels, particularly among low income and rural populations. Per capita caloric/protein availability declined by 1.3% annually between 1967 and 1979.[12] The differential impact of the decline in food availability and corresponding food price increases on different income groups and regions was also notable. In the wealthy region of São Paulo, cassava, beans, and maize were among the five foods with the largest retail price increases. In the poorest region of the northeast, cassava and bean prices registered the greatest increases. Low income families in the northeast have been the hardest hit by the soybean revolution in Brazil (Homem de Melo 1986:48–51).

Brazil provides an important example of how government-supported modernization and export promotion of agriculture has contributed to economic growth with increased polarization among different social groups and regions. The substitution of grains in production is part of a much broader, complex process of development. Land concentration and landlessness have increased in recent decades, income inequalities in rural areas have risen, low income and rural populations face precarious food supplies and inflated prices, and the country as a whole spends increasing quantities of precious foreign earnings on food imports.

Peru

As in Brazil, major food crops in Peru include roots, tubers (particularly potatoes), and pulses, as well as basic grains. We therefore include in our analysis an examination of the shifts in cultivation of these noncereal crops. Small-scale producers in the Sierra grow potatoes for use as a food, rotated with barley, a winter cash crop cultivated for use by beer breweries. The soft maize that is cultivated in the Sierra, also for direct food consumption, represents approximately one-half of all maize grown in Peru. The other half, known as hard yellow maize, provides a major source of animal feed in the country. Formerly concentrated on the coastal plains, hard yellow maize cultivation has increasingly shifted inland to the jungle areas. On the coast, rice has taken the place of hard yellow maize.

In Peru, per capita cereal production in general, and maize output in particular, has not kept pace with population growth since 1961. While the population grew at 2.8% per year between 1961 and 1986, overall cereal production and maize production both grew at 2.3%, leaving a shortfall of 0.5% per year. This picture is even more discouraging, however, because much of the increase in maize production has been of hard maize for animal feed. Soft maize production, which in Peru and Ecuador (Chiriboga 1988:424) is produced on small farms of less than 5 hectares, actually declined substantially. Grain production as a proportion of overall cultivated area remained relatively constant.

The output and area dedicated to potatoes suffered an absolute decline between 1963 and 1983. Area harvested actually rose in the 1960s, from 231,309 hectares to a high of 320,050 hectares in 1971. Acreage then dropped by more than 50%, to 150,446 total hectares in 1983. Increasing yields made up for some of the loss in acreage, but total production in 1983 was still below that of 1963. Average area harvested for

1963–1966 was 252,422 hectares, declining to 190,220 in 1980–1983. This represents annual growth rates of –1.5% in area and 1.9% in yields, leaving production stagnant (Paz Silva 1986:110). This same pattern of declining production of potatoes is found in Ecuador. Larger farmers have replaced potatoes with pasture for livestock production. Just during the years between 1968 and 1975, for example, the amount of pasture in Ecuador doubled to over 3.5 million hectares (Chiriboga 1988:435). Although we do not have comparable data for Peru, indications are that similar processes occurred there.

A more detailed analysis of cereal production reveals that, although the acreage covered by all grains remained relatively unchanged between 1961 and 1986, the composition of grain production shifted substantially. In Peru, while the proportion of land dedicated to rice has jumped two and a half times, that in maize cultivation has remained relatively unchanged, and wheat and barley have suffered major declines (see Table XVII). Barley fell at a rate of 2.8% per year. While substantial research expenditures have supported experiments on producing disease resistant and high yielding varieties of rice, the Ministry of Agriculture has not made barley a priority, "despite its large crop area and the fact that it is a staple food in the Sierra" (Paz Silva 1986:46–47).

Rice acreage grew from 10% of the total cereal area in 1961–1965 to 26% in 1981–1985. Wheat and barley dropped proportionately, from 20% to 11% and from 23% to 14% of the total, respectively (see Table VI). While the share of maize cultivation in grain area increased slightly, from 43.2% to 45.2%, poor yields relative to rice meant that the share of maize in total cereal production dropped from 41.5% to 36.7% between 1961–1965 and 1981–1985. This occurred, apparently, because the cultivation of hard yellow maize grown for animal feed shifted from the more fertile coastal area to the more marginal jungle, where yields are lower, and was replaced by rice on the coast. Yields of maize in the jungle averaged 50% of coastal yields for the 25-year period. By contrast, yields of soft maize grown in the Sierra averaged 1,009 kg/ha between 1964 and 1984, or about two-thirds of jungle yields and slightly more than one-third of coastal yields (Paz Silva 1986).

While government price support and other policies have encouraged rice and maize production increases, they have discouraged wheat output. With domestic wheat priced higher than international wheat (and higher than domestic rice), and with national milling interests preferring the higher quality international wheat over the domestic, wheat production has declined from 13% of total cereal production to 5% between 1961–1965 and 1981–1985. An overvalued currency has further encouraged imports. As a result of the combined changes in production and government policies, grain imports have almost tripled in volume in the 25-year period reviewed here. During 1981–1985, imports averaged 72% of cereal output, up from 40% in the 1961–1965 period.

These shifts in food production in Peru raise a number of questions for producer and consumer welfare that require further research. The data suggest that only small-scale producers are continuing production of potatoes and barley in the Sierra; larger farmers have shifted to more profitable activities related to livestock production. There are other questions for which we would like answers. For example, what has happened to wheat producers, given the shrinkage of acreage dedicated to wheat cultivation? The impact on producers and consumers of the substitution of rice for hard yellow maize also requires further research. Who are the rice producers compared to the former maize producers? Is the substitution of rice for animal feed a positive or negative trend for the bulk of the country's consumers?

These and other questions need to be addressed in a more detailed study of the distributional impacts on Peru's population of the transformations that have occurred in agriculture in the past. Given the turmoil that has enveloped the country in the late 1980s as a result of the Shining Path and Tupac Amaru guerrilla movements, we would expect further declines in agricultural production and increases in food imports.

4

The Substitution of Grains
in Northern Africa
and the Middle East

REGIONAL OVERVIEW

The dramatic expansion in oil production in the Middle East and northern Africa has been the single most important factor stimulating change in agricultural production, consumption, and trade since the 1970s. According to Khaldi's (1984) comprehensive study of the region, the sudden increase in availability of oil dollars led to major increases in demand for and consumption of food, particularly livestock products, in the oil states.[13] To a lesser extent, increased earnings from abroad also generated higher food demand and consumption in the labor-exporting states such as Egypt. Other food-producing states in the region did not benefit directly from oil revenues but were indirectly affected through the reorientation of their agricultural sectors.

Khaldi's study provides complementary material that is of particular interest to us and will be reviewed here in some detail.[14] According to the Khaldi report, the indirect result of the oil boom has been a major shift in land use patterns away from traditional staples and toward livestock-oriented production. Between 1973 and 1980, the production of staple cereals was stagnant in oil-producing countries (with an annual growth rate of 0.3%) and declined on the average in the labor-exporting countries at a rate of 0.5%. And while cereal production averaged a 1.6% annual increase in food-producing countries, noncereal production rose more than twice as fast, at 3.6% per year. Moreover, meat production increased at 5.5% in the oil states, 1.3% in the labor-exporting nations, and 4% in the food-producing countries (Khaldi 1984:16–25). As examples of this phenomenon, we review the data from each of the three types of economies: Algeria, an oil exporter; Egypt, a labor exporter; and Morocco and Turkey, both primarily food producers.

From 1973 to 1980, the annual growth in the consumption of food staples grew at a rate of 5.1% in the oil states; 3.3% in the labor-exporting countries; and 2.8% in the food-producing countries. The use of staples for feed grew at a much faster and unequal rate: 9.4% in the first group; 8.1% in the second; and 5.4% in the third. Similarly, meat consumption in oil-exporting nations rose at a rate of 12.7% per year; in labor-exporting countries at 4.6%; and in food-producing countries at 4.1% (Khaldi 1984:16–25).[15]

Because domestic production has failed to keep pace with regional demand, food imports have risen many times. Moreover, the composition of imports has shifted to include a much higher percentage of livestock products and feed grains. Imports of meat rose at a rate of 22% per year in the oil states and 11% annually in the labor-exporting states (Paulino 1986:26). That is, more food has been imported to meet the demands of middle and upper income groups than to provide staple food grains to the bulk of the population. Regional food imports are projected to be the highest in the world by the year 2000 (Khaldi 1984).

Thus, the FAO supply utilization data clearly show that with the increased integration of this area into the global oil market, staple food production has stagnated, grains are increasingly used for animal feed rather than direct human consumption, and regional food self-sufficiency has declined. The statistics suggest that these changes are accompanied by serious negative effects on producer and consumer welfare.

The data also indicate that at least some of the important changes in agriculture are occurring not through shifts in production of different kinds of grains, but shifts in grain utilization. For example, while maize is a traditional food grain in the areas of Egypt where it is produced, recent increases in maize production and imports in Egypt are destined almost entirely for animal feed. Thus, the supply utilization data in some cases highlight more clearly the important changes that are occurring in food production and consumption patterns. These data also show how the growth of food grain staples has lagged behind livestock production.

The findings of our study, based on country-level analysis of FAO production and trade data, are generally consistent with the above findings but show some important country variations and raise some additional questions. In Table XVIII, we see the pattern of grain substitution in production in Algeria, Egypt, Morocco, and Turkey between 1961–1965 and 1981–1985. It is evident that considerable shifts have occurred in crop cultivation within the grain sector.

While each country varies in the specific kinds of changes that have occurred in agricultural production, consumption, and trade, they also share certain common features. Wheat is the primary cereal staple in most of northern Africa. In the countries included in this study, its share of cultivated area is stagnant or declining, although increasing yields have made up for some of the loss of acreage. Moreover, in each country, staple cropland has been increasingly lost to livestock-oriented production. Other declining staple cereals include sorghum and millet in Egypt. Barley in Algeria and Morocco and maize in Egypt are both feed grains and food grains. Although the acreage and output of these crops are growing, it appears that much of that increase is in response to their expanding use for feed rather than human food. On a regional level, the use of coarse grains (all grains except wheat and rice) for feed increased at a rate of 7.5% per year between 1973 and 1980, while feed use increased at 1.7%.

In Table XIX, we summarize the changing composition of grain imports to these countries between 1961–1965 and 1981–1985. The common pattern that emerges for Algeria, Egypt, and Morocco, is that maize imports are rising relative to other grains. Imported maize to these countries is used entirely for animal feed.

COUNTRY ANALYSES

Turkey

Turkey, in contrast to the countries previously discussed, has succeeded in attaining food self-sufficiency and has become, since the mid-1970s, a substantial grain exporter (see Table XX). It is the only country in this study that has made the transition from net food importer to exporter. Thus, Turkey has not followed the regional pattern, identified by Khaldi, of stagnation in the food grain sector accompanied by increasing food imports.

Domestic cereal production has slightly outpaced population growth, and per capita cereal supply has grown at 1.1% per year.

Turkey achieved dramatic increases in wheat output primarily through a green revolution in production technology: the introduction of high yielding varieties of wheat, the application of fertilizers and other chemical inputs, the mechanization of production, and the construction of irrigation projects. Thus, yields grew at an annual rate of 2.4% between 1961 and 1986, averaging 1.5 tons/ha. Cultivated acreage also expanded, averaging 61% of cereal land in 1961–1965 and growing to 68% in 1981–1985. See Table XXI for a summary of the annual growth rates for average area, yields, and production of these grains for the 25-year period.

The social and economic impacts of this technological revolution on different income groups may be understood only through more detailed case studies. Although grain exports finally exceeded imports in the mid-1970s, Turkey continues to import substantial quantities of grains, primarily rice. A fuller review should examine supply utilization and food consumption data, as well as changes in the nongrain agricultural sector. It is doubtful that the country's food or nutritional problems are solved. Turkey does, however, provide an example of how policies that support technological advances in the grain sector may move a country toward food self-sufficiency.

Algeria

The production of barley, used for direct food consumption and animal feed in Algeria, has been increasing over the past 25 years (see Table XXII). Between 1961 and 1986, barley acreage increased from 29% to 34% of the cultivated land while wheat declined from 69% to 61% (see Table XVIII). The pattern of barley supplanting wheat is clearer from 1966 on, when barley reached a low of 24% of the total cultivated area, and wheat, a high of 74%.[16] The increase in barley production in contrast to wheat is more striking if yields are taken into consideration: Barley yields increased at 1.9% annually as opposed to 1% for wheat. Consequently, barley production rose from 27% of total grain production in 1961–1965 (24% in 1966–1970) to 38% in 1981–1985. Wheat dropped from 71% (73% in 1966–1970) to 58% during the same period.[17]

The relationship between these agricultural changes and the

welfare of agricultural producers in Algeria is unclear. Who are the traditional producers of barley versus wheat? In what regions are they located? Have traditional wheat growers shifted to barley, or do the two crops involve substantially different systems of production and technological inputs?

Although the impact of shifting patterns of food production on domestic consumption are not self-evident, the data in this study do show that Algeria has experienced a serious erosion in per capita food supply during this period. This may be related to the singular importance of the oil industry in the country's economy. Although the government of Algeria established food self-sufficiency as a national goal in more recent years, for the period under review here neither cereal production nor supply kept pace with population growth. The annual growth rates of per capita cereal production and supply are −1.7% and −7% respectively for the 25-year period. Algeria's decline in per capita food supply is the highest of any country in this study.

These developments in production had an important impact on Algeria's participation in international markets. In the early 1960s, Algeria exported substantial amounts of barley and wheat, which respectively composed 59% and 38% of all grain exports. But by the early 1970s, grain exports were insignificant; they declined to zero by the early 1980s. Grain imports grew by almost tenfold in the same interval.

Morocco

In contrast to Algeria, food production is a substantial part of Morocco's economy. The changing trends in agricultural production are also more variable. In Table XXIII, we summarize the annual growth rates for average area, yields, and production of the important grains for the 25-year period. While output of barley grew steadily from 42% to 48% of total grain production in 1961–1980 (in keeping with a corresponding expansion in cultivated area), barley production declined to 43% of total cereal production in the 1980s. Barley yields averaged 0.9 ton/ha and grew at an average of only 1.1% per year. By contrast, wheat yields averaged 1 ton/ha and increased at 2.4% annually. Thus, although there was no additional land dedicated to wheat, total production of wheat climbed from 42% to 48% of total grain output between 1961 and 1985.

Again, the impacts of these agricultural changes on the

domestic population require additional detailed research. The Moroccan government established national policies to expand food production, but despite these efforts, Morocco increased grain imports sixfold between 1961 and 1986. The composition of grain imports also changed, with maize replacing barley imports. Exports of maize, barley, and wheat, which averaged 126,000 tons in the period 1961–1965, declined to virtually nothing by the 1976–1980 period. Unlike Algeria, however, Morocco has managed to keep cereal production marginally ahead of population growth: Per capita cereal supply has grown at an annual rate of 1.3%.

Recent government policy has focused on attempts to reduce imports, feed the cities, and accelerate the integration of farmers into the market. Part of these efforts have involved the substitution of one kind of wheat for another. Farmers in Morocco have generally planted durum (a hard, tough) wheat, most of which was grown for their own consumption. Government policy has been to encourage the production of bread wheat on irrigated schemes; currently, efforts are under way to expand production to rainfed areas of the country. Thus, in this case, the substitution of grains has been to replace the type of wheat grown and eaten by small farmers with another type of wheat that is more suitable for making bread, favored by urban consumers. There has been a lack of incentives for barley production, so it appears that the decline in production of this grain will continue (Ahmed Herzenni, Ministry of Agriculture official, personal communication).

Egypt

Egypt is one of the few countries in this study that has experienced a net decrease in per capita grain production since the 1960s. While population growth has advanced at a rate of 2.4% annually, cereal output grew at 1.6% per year. The increases in grain output that did occur were entirely due to the growth of yields. The gap has been made up for by grain imports (primarily wheat, but increasingly maize) that averaged a 23% annual growth rate for the entire period. A comparison of growth rates by decades, however, demonstrates that the relative decline in production and increase in imports has accelerated since the 1970s. As a number of studies have shown, government policies have been instrumental in the transformation of food production and consumption patterns in recent decades (Alderman and von Braun 1984; Scobie 1981, 1983; von Braun and de Haen 1983).

The basic staple foods in Egypt are wheat, maize, rice, sorghum, millet, and pulses (mainly broad beans). Cereals constitute 66.7% of the average caloric and protein intake of the population; pulses make up 3.7% of caloric and 10.2% of protein intake. Consumption patterns vary according to income and rural or urban residence, and they have been changing over time. Maize, sorghum, and millet, along with beans, are traditional subsistence foods grown and consumed by small producers. Maize has historically been grown in the delta and in middle Egypt; sorghum and millet are produced in Upper Egypt (the south). Rice was introduced and promoted as an export crop for which Egypt has a comparative advantage in production, but increasing urban incomes now purchase virtually all of the rice domestically produced. Wheat, available at subsidized prices even in rural areas, has replaced a large portion of maize for human consumption, particularly in the last decade. Maize, once primarily a human food, now constitutes 75% of the animal feed produced domestically (Gardner and Parker 1985).

In the last 25 years, maize acreage and output have expanded in response to the demand for animal feed, while other food grains, including wheat, rice, sorghum, and millet, have suffered a relative decline in their share of total grain production. As indicated in Table XXIV, these trends in acreage have been accompanied by similar patterns in yields and output. The average annual growth rates of maize yields surpassed those of wheat, rice, sorghum, and millet. Total maize production grew at three times the annual rate of wheat and rice, while sorghum and millet suffered absolute declines.[18]

Dramatic changes in Egypt's grain trade have accompanied the shifts in the composition of food production. Egypt was a net exporter of wheat through the 1940s and self-sufficient until the mid-1950s. By the 1980s, it was the world's third-largest importer, behind the USSR and China. Egypt was self-sufficient in maize until the 1960s; despite expanding production, imports now account for 43% of production (1981–1985). Egypt was a major exporter of rice until the 1980s, but imports are projected as necessary in the future. Since the mid-1970s, Egypt's self-sufficiency in pulses, an important element in domestic diets, has decreased to 75% (Gardner and Parker 1985:24–33).

The first major changes in production patterns can be traced to World War II, when Egypt substantially decreased its traditional cultivation of cotton for export and expanded cereal production in response to the consumption needs of the British army in northern Africa. While cotton production slowly regained its prior levels, and by the early 1950s surpassed them because of the demand stimulated by the Korean War, cereal production, particularly of wheat, remained significant. Agricultural productivity continued to increase owing to policies instituted by the Nasser administration following the 1952 revolution. The land reform program, for example, which redistributed 12.5% of the land and affected 340,000 families, led to more intensive cultivation. The construction of the Aswan Dam provided the opportunity for some significant shifts in land utilization, particularly in the expansion of rice and sugar cultivation, and the increase in maize yields by 40%. Rice acreage expanded by 519,000 hectares, and sugar by over 88,000. And the availability of irrigation allowed maize farmers to plant their crops earlier (in May or June, rather than in July), thereby taking more advantage of summer heat and light and avoiding the maize borer. The failure to deal with drainage problems, however, led to serious salinity problems affecting 35% of the cultivated area, according to the FAO. These technical problems, along with the impact of government policies, led to significant production shifts beginning in the 1960s and continuing to the present (Richards 1982:168–196).

Government production and consumption policies since the 1950s and 1960s have been aimed at subsidizing industrialization through low producer prices, supporting the production of export crops to earn foreign exchange, and providing inexpensive food to urban workers and consumers. While some crops are highly regulated and marketed only through the government, others are completely unregulated. Cotton, the primary export crop until the 1970s, is the most regulated crop, produced under a quota system with free irrigation and inputs controlled and subsidized by the government, and sold only to the government at prices fixed below market and international prices. Cotton and cotton seed production declined in absolute terms between 1969 and 1981 (Gardner and Parker 1985:13).

Wheat and rice, also grown under government quotas with free irrigation, and controlled, subsidized inputs, are slightly less regulated than is cotton in terms of marketing: While a portion of these cereal crops must be sold to the government, the remainder may be sold in the free market. Government prices are fixed considerably below market and international prices. In 1981, for example, wheat and rice were priced at 21% and 15% below the market price, respectively. Unregulated crops are also grown with subsidized inputs but sold only in the free market. These include maize, sugar, berseem (or birsim) clover, most fruits and vegetables, and livestock products (Gardner and Parker 1985:20–21).[19] The impact of price and other regulations on the agricultural decisionmaking of producers has been striking.[20] As one researcher notes:

Because of distortions resulting from price regulations, farmers have often preferred to cultivate non-regulated crops. . .

Farmers have diverted fertilizers and reduced compulsory plantings of controlled crops. Such cutbacks risk fines, but apparently farmers have determined that the extra profits are worth the risk.

> slivestock production is uncontrolled and provides high returns, forages like berseem clover, maize, and wheat straw have been lucrative crops for farmers. At times, the free market price of wheat straw is above that of wheat grain. As a result, feed crops have occupied a growing portion of the cropped area, and the foodgrain area has declined (Richards 1982:247).

Price policies throughout the 1960s and 1970s penalized wheat and rice (as well as cotton) producers, with the result that farmers shifted production from cereals, noncereal foods, and cotton for export to livestock and horticultural products, destined for upper class urban diets and, since the 1970s, for export to wealthy oil states. Maize, once penalized as a food crop, has grown in importance with the expansion of the livestock industry.

Food grains compete directly with feed and export-oriented crops for limited agricultural land. Among winter crops, grown between November and mid-May, the less profitable wheat and broad bean crops compete with berseem clover and vegetables for available land. Clover, a nitrogen-fixing crop that precedes cotton planting, covers 50% of the winter cropland. In the summer (mid-May through August), rice, maize, cotton, and vegetables compete. Maize is the predominant crop in the "Nili" season—from August to October (Gardner and Parker 1985:13).

Food production has suffered in two respects: in relation to total cultivated area and in the substitution of individual grains in production. The area devoted to cereals as a whole has declined relative to more profitable crops such as berseem clover, fruits and vegetables, and soybeans. Between 1950–1954 and 1978, for example, berseem clover increased from 23% to 26% of the total cultivated area (Richards 1982:219). Soybean cultivation, although still relatively minor, grew from 2,000 to 75,000 hectares between 1974 and 1983 (Gardner and Parker 1985:34).

With respect to the substitution of grains in production, wheat, rice, sorghum, and millet have declined in relation to the expansion of maize in response to the demand for feed. Wheat has decreased from 30% to 27% of the grain area; sorghum and millet have dropped from 11% to 8%. Since 1966–1970, rice acreage has declined from 24% of the area to 20%. Notably, production of maize, destined for human consumption, was declining relatively until the mid-1960s (from 37% to 34% of the cereal acreage). From 1966–1970 on, however, with the growth in the livestock industry, maize cultivation has expanded from 34% of the cereal area to 42% in 1981–1985.

While clover supplies enough fodder for approximately one-half the year, there has been a growing shortage of fodder in Egypt. As a result, one practice that has increased is the stripping of maize plants for fodder, a practice thought to reduce yields (Richards 1982:219). Feed is in such great demand that Egypt imported fodder for the first time in 1984 (Gardner and Parker 1985:34).

As a result of the transformation in agricultural production, the volume of food imports to Egypt has grown fourfold in the 25 years under review, and almost threefold since 1970–1975. Grain imports rose from 2 million tons in 1961–1965 to 2.8 million in 1971–1975, and to 8 million in 1981–1985. Imports equaled one-third of cereal production in 1961–1965 and 94% in 1981–1985. While wheat continues to dominate imports, its share has declined from 89% to 81% in the 25-year period. Maize for animal feed has climbed from 5.5% of grain imports in 1966–1970 to 19.1% in 1981–1985.

Egypt's controversial food subsidy program, initiated in the 1950s as an important part of the social reform effort, has become increasingly dependent on food imports, particularly wheat, to meet its expanding needs. As a result, the program now consumes 10–15% of the total Egyptian budget (von Braun and de Haen 1983). The expansion is due in part to the expanding population and in part to the extension of coverage to additional foods in the 1970s. Over 92% of Egypt's population, both rural and urban, participates in the program. Central to the program is the provision of wheat flour and wheat bread to consumers in unlimited quantities at approximately 30% of cost. While some foods, such as meat and fish, reach only upper income groups, the program as a whole is more beneficial to poor people (Alderman and von Braun 1984). However, producers suffer an implicit tax on their commodities as a result of the pricing program.

The major surge in imports, since 1970–1975, corresponds to the period following the initiation of the "open door policy" in 1973, the attempt by the Sadat government to encourage foreign and domestic private investment and create a free foreign exchange market. While gross domestic product (GDP) grew by almost 6% from 1975 on, the economic expansion was at the expense of heavy government spending financed by concessional foreign credit. The increasing trade deficit led to a negative trade balance of U.S. $3.6 billion in 1979, despite enormous increases in the remittances from workers in the oil-producing states of the Gulf during the 1970s.[21] In the agricultural sector, the trade balance went from a $300 million surplus in 1970 to a $2.5 billion deficit in 1981.

During the same period, the volume of grain exports declined from 343,000 metric tons in 1961–1965 to 44,000 in 1981–1985. Egypt's current grain exports equal 13% of their total volume in 1961–1965. The value of Egypt's net grain deficit has grown from $93 million in 1961–1965 to $1.6 billion in 1981–1985. Despite massive food imports, however, malnutrition is a widespread problem, particularly in rural areas. Forty-two percent of the population suffers a caloric shortfall of 20% of the amount required to renew daily energy, while the nonpoor enjoy a surplus of 31% of their daily requirements, according to a 1977 survey. The bottom 20% of the population suffers caloric deficiencies of 35% or more. That study also found that the protein intake of the poor was only 76% of the daily level recommended by the FAO (Radwan and Lee 1986).[22]

Food grains compose over two-thirds of the caloric intake of the Egyptian population, and the percentage is even higher among low income groups. With income distribution and food consumption among income groups highly unequal, government price policies that support the commercial production of feed grains over food staples clearly exacerbate these inequalities. The growth of maize and clover for animal feed and the expansion of the livestock sector, while serving the needs of the bulk of the population, do not help the country achieve food self-sufficiency or contribute to the economic stability of Egypt's external position. Instead, these trends have contributed to increasingly unequal distribution of resources, widespread malnutrition among low income populations, and destabilizing foreign debt.

5

The Substitution of Grains in Western Africa

In this chapter we examine two countries in western Africa, Burkina Faso and Nigeria. Their commonality lies in the types of basic food crops that small producers there have traditionally grown: sorghum and millet, maize, root crops, and legumes. Their development over the past 25 years is so radically different, however, that it is important to understand the varying processes that have affected their agricultural sectors.

COUNTRY ANALYSES

Burkina Faso

More than 80% of cropland in Burkina Faso is devoted to the subsistence production of basic staples, including sorghum, millet, maize, root crops, and legumes. Traditional production systems intercrop sorghum and millet with root crops and legumes, mainly cassava, yams, and *niebe*, a type of grain legume. Between 1961 and 1986, cereal cultivation covered over 2 million hectares or approximately 76% of the average of 2.6 million hectares of total cropland. Sorghum production accounted for an average of 51% of cereal cultivation, while millet averaged 39%. Maize, a minor crop, covered an additional 7% of cereal acreage.

Burkina Faso is one of the poorest countries in Africa, and

65

one of the most severely affected by the Sahelian drought of 1968–1974 and the drought of the 1980s. Crop failure, decimation of pastoralists' herds, famine, widespread migration, and massive international aid have characterized these periods (Binns 1986:248). Examination of FAO statistics on grain cultivation and production, however, show relatively little variation between years of drought and years of normal rainfall, as is indicated in Table XXV.

It is clear, however, that major increases in grain imports occurred during the drought years: Imports doubled between 1966–1970 and 1971–1975, and rose by another 50% between 1976–1980 and 1981–1985. Low yields and low growth rates in yields characterize all grain production, as is evident in Table XXVI.

A number of factors have contributed to the limited growth in domestic grain production: low seasonal rainfall coupled with periods of drought, poor soils, low technological development, and high population density (22–25 persons per square kilometer)—one of the highest rural population densities in Africa. Onchocerciasis or "river blindness," a disease prevalent in the river valleys and affecting approximately one-tenth of the country's land area, has prohibited use of this fertile land for food production. An Onchocerciasis Control Program, established by the government in the 1970s with the assistance of international research institutes, bilateral aid agencies, and the World Bank, sought to eradicate the disease and resettle a number of river valleys. In villages where resettlement has occurred, this development effort has shown considerable promise for improving food production, even though it may not yet be reflected in national-level production statistics (McMillan 1987).

Unlike most countries considered here, the shares of major staple grains in overall cereal cultivation increased slightly in Burkina Faso relative to less important and nontraditional grains. Millet expanded from 38% to 42% of the area between 1961–1965 and 1981–1985; maize declined from 8% to 6% and rice from 2.3% to 1.3%. The share of cereal cultivation in overall harvested area, however, has declined at a rate of 0.4% per year since 1961. Overall food crops (including cereal and noncereal crops) grew at a rate of 2% between 1969–1971 and 1977–1980, while nonfood crops increased at a rate of 7.2%.

Expanding cotton cultivation was primarily responsible for the growth of nonfood crops. Cotton, Burkina Faso's most important export crop, expanded from 23,000 hectares in 1961 to 75,000 in 1979. Output grew from 23,000 to 80,000 metric tons in the same period. Other important export and cash crops include nuts (karite, cashew, and groundnuts), sugar, and fruits and vegetables. Livestock raising, also a major part of the agricultural sector, accounts for approximately 25% of exports. It does not compete with cropland, however, because over 90% of the stocks are ruminants on free range land in the Sahelian north, Sudanian center, and Guinean south (World Bank 1983:10–12).

Some evidence suggests that a regression in food production preceded the 1972 drought and was caused by government policies that favored export agriculture, particularly cotton, over food crops. Government officials have viewed cotton production, begun in 1950 by the Compagnie Française pour le Developpement des Fibres Textiles (CFDT), as the principal source of foreign exchange. Following the 1972 drought, however, international aid agencies, including the World Bank, began promoting "integrated rural development" projects to improve small producer food crop production through the provision of credit, guaranteed adequate producer prices, and modernization in cultivation through the use of improved seeds and technical inputs (Gervais 1984:130–133). The Onchocerciasis Control Program is another example of these efforts.

In the 1980s, cereal production continues to occupy almost 75% of the country's arable land and to account for 80% of the value of agricultural production. The 2.6% annual growth rate in cereal production has also kept ahead of the population growth rate of 2%, lower than that of any other African country in our study and the result, in part, of significant outmigration of workers to neighboring countries.

Despite a stable preponderance of land devoted to food grains and noncereal staples, however, the volume of food imports to Burkina Faso has steadily increased since 1961. Burkina Faso's net grain trade balance has steadily deteriorated: from U.S. $856,000 in 1961–1965 to U.S. $12.2 million in 1981–1985. Clearly, the two major droughts coupled with the already poor conditions that the country suffers are major contributing factors. But while the volume of grain imports has increased sixfold in the last 25 years, imports still equal only 4.8% of domestic cereal production (up from 1% in 1961–1965).

In addition, when grain imports have been necessary, they have been made up increasingly of traditional staples, particularly maize and sorghum. Maize and sorghum imports have grown over twice as fast as those of wheat, the other major grain import, consumed mainly by the middle and upper income urban population. Thus, wheat has decreased its share of grain imports from 94% in 1966–1970 to 52% in 1981–1985. By contrast, maize has grown from 6% to 23% of the grain imports, and sorghum, from zero to 25%.

Burkina Faso has maintained a surprising level of self-sufficiency in food, in light of the country's severe impoverishment and natural calamities. Moreover, shortfalls in production have been compensated by the increase in the importation of food grains that are oriented toward a majority of the population, rather than largely upper income groups. Since the 1984 revolution, the government has moved toward a policy of food self-sufficiency. Given that daily per capita caloric intake is roughly 79% of nutritional requirements (Vermeer 1983:77), however, the government's task is a particularly difficult one.

In order to implement its goal of food self-sufficiency, the government nationalized land, increased producer prices on cash and food crops, doubled agriculture's share of the national budget, and attempted to increase cereal production through a subsidized fertilizer program (Hodgkinson 1987:280). The impact of these policies on the welfare of the bulk of the population is yet to be determined.

Nigeria

Nigeria presents a case study at the opposite extreme from that of Burkina Faso. Here, as in other oil-exporting countries, the explosion of the oil industry has radically altered the agricultural sector in the last 25 years. Oil contributed 3% to total export earnings in 1960, 60% in 1970, 93% in 1975, and 96% in 1980 (Andrae and Beckman 1985:4). As a result, both food and export crop cultivation have been neglected. Agricultural export commodities, including palm oil, cotton, peanuts, bananas, and cocoa, made up the majority of export earnings in 1960. Only cocoa continues to be of importance in the 1980s (Mabbs-Zeno 1986:5).

Similarly, the area dedicated to basic food staples has also declined. Forty percent of the caloric intake of Nigerians comes from grains, according to FAO estimates. Sorghum and millet are the main cereal staples in the north, while maize is the basic grain in the south. An additional 30% of caloric consumption comes from root crops, primarily cassava and yams grown in the south, and cocoyams (taro) produced in the southwest. They constitute almost two-thirds of the volume of agricultural production, but output of these basic foods dropped by over 30% between 1969 and 1981 (Andrae and Beckman 1985). Most of these basic foods are consumed by the producer and never reach formal marketing structures. According to a 1975 government survey, this held true for 90% of the sorghum and millet grown in Nigeria (Mabbs-Zeno 1986:8–9, 21).[23]

Total cereal cultivation has declined by almost 20%, from 11.1 million hectares in 1961–1965 to 9.1 million hectares in 1981–1985. During the same period, the country has also undergone substitution of grains in production, with the traditional staples of sorghum, millet, and maize displaced by expanding rice cultivation. In Table XXVII, we summarize the relative growth rates of cereal grains in Nigeria for the period under review. The share of cultivated area in maize has dropped from 12% to 6%. By contrast, rice production, which responds to growing middle and upper income markets and which is cultivated in the fertile river valleys through government subsidies, has grown from 1.6% to 7% of the harvested grain area. Acreage in sorghum and millet has fluctuated. The share of sorghum fell from 47% of total grain land in 1961–1965 to 41% in 1971–1975, before recovering to 45% in 1981–1985. Millet cultivation rose from 39% of the total in 1961–1965 to 45% in 1971–1975, and then declined to 41% in 1981–1985.

Cereal production and supply have not kept pace with population growth in Nigeria in the last 25 years. Per capita production has declined at a rate of 1.9% per year, and per capita supply at 1.3% annually, despite substantial increases in food imports.

As a result of the dramatic expansion of the oil industry and the potential it held as the main source of the country's economic growth, Nigeria dramatically increased its dependence on oil export earnings over the past 25 years, while neglecting other sectors of the economy. Agriculture was relatively ignored, the 1967 Civil War and subsequent droughts exacerbated already deteriorating domestic food production, and Nigeria became dependent on food imports. Oil dollars replaced export agriculture and financed the inflow of food.

By the mid-1970s, the government began paying more serious attention to agriculture, notably in its third (1975–1980) and fourth (1980–1985) Five Year Development plans. The budget for agriculture rose to ₦2.3 billion in the third plan and ₦8 billion in the fourth, although the collapse in oil prices after 1981 subsequently reduced the latter amount (Roy 1987:5).

State intervention in agriculture followed three main strategies: (1) large-scale irrigation programs administered through 11 River Basin Development authorities; (2) large-scale mechanized food farms owned and operated by the state in conjunction with foreign agribusiness; and (3) integrated rural agricultural development projects to promote green revolution smallholder production modeled on prototypes developed by the World Bank in the early 1970s in the rich northern farming regions of Funtua, Gusau, and Bauchi (Watts 1987:77–81).

The government-sponsored irrigation projects were largely designed to develop import-substituting production of wheat and rice. But despite huge expenditures, rice and wheat yields and production remained low, costs of production were uncompetitively high, and ecological and salinization problems as well as local peasant resistance continued to plague irrigation efforts. Similarly, the state farms have faced skyrocketing costs, technical difficulties, administrative corruption, and waning foreign interest, with the result that many have been scaled down or abandoned. The smallholder strategy, developed since 1980, has consisted of a subsidized package of improved seed varieties and chemical and mechanical inputs (fertilizers, insecticides, plows, tractors) funded in part by the World Bank and administered to producers through a parastatal agency. These projects targeted 60,000 to 80,000 small producers to improve food production, primarily of sorghum and maize. While initial reviews suggest that this strategy has the best potential for improving food output, it also appears to target more commercialized farmers with holdings in excess of 20 hectares, thereby raising the potential of increasing polarization in the rural areas (Watts 1987).

In the meantime, grain imports to Nigeria have risen faster than those to any other country in our study: from 72,000 metric tons in 1961–1965 to 1.8 million tons in 1981–1985. Until 1975, wheat imports accounted for 98% of all grain imports. Since then, maize and rice have been imported in substantial amounts. Maize imports, destined entirely for animal feed in response to growing urban demand for meat, grew at a rate of 30% per year and now make up 7% of all grain imports. Rice imports, destined for the urban market, increased at 26% annually and now equal 25% of all grain imports. Wheat imports grew at 12.5% and currently constitute 66% of the total (see Table XXX). While Nigeria was virtually self-sufficient in cereal production in 1961–1965 (when imports were less than 1% of production), imports equaled 20% of domestic production in the 1981–1985 period.

The heavy dependence on food imports, however, particularly wheat, put a serious burden on export earnings when oil exports and prices began their decline after 1979. Responding to the financial crisis following the military coup of 1983, the new government issued an austerity budget, curtailing food imports, particularly of rice and maize. Wheat imports, however, were maintained as a priority item, "since bread has become the cheapest staple food of our people."[24] Thus, grain imports continue to drain foreign exchange earnings. The value of Nigeria's net grain trade balance deteriorated from a negative U.S. $12.6 million in 1961–1965 to U.S. $67.4 million in 1971–1975. In the 1976–1980 period, it reached U.S. $458.3 million, and in 1981–1985, U.S. $614.3 million (see Table XXXI).

6

The Substitution of Grains in Eastern and Southern Africa

REGIONAL OVERVIEW

The countries of eastern and southern Africa included in this study vary considerably in the kind and extent of change they are experiencing in agricultural production. As in northern Africa, in some countries one food grain is displacing another in terms of its share in acreage and production, and the significance of the change is not entirely apparent. This is true in the case of Ethiopia. It also applies to the changing patterns of maize, sorghum, and millet cultivation in Kenya, Tanzania, and Zimbabwe. There are also some common patterns: Wheat and rice cultivation, geared toward urban middle and upper income diets, is increasing relative to staple grains in Sudan, South Africa, and Tanzania. Grains that are expanding in acreage (maize, sorghum, wheat, and rice) are also those that are being exported in increasing amounts by Kenya, Tanzania, Zimbabwe, and South Africa.

The relative changes in cereal cultivation in these countries are presented in Table XXVIII. Taking yields into consideration, the trends in total output for these cereals correspond to the increases and decreases in acreage cultivated. That is, the changes in acreage rather than yields account for the bulk of shifting production.[25]

In Ethiopia, there was a slight shift from wheat to maize production during the 25-year period, but it would appear that this small change is not significant in terms of producer and consumer welfare. There were, however, corresponding increases in domestic maize consumption. Maize as a percentage of per

73

capita caloric intake grew from 15% to 18% between 1961–1965 and 1975–1977 (CIMMYT 1984).

In Sudan, wheat production for middle and upper income consumption expanded rapidly between 1961 and 1980 relative to sorghum, the country's main staple cereal. In the 1980s, however, this trend was reversed as a result of changes in government policies.

For Kenya, Tanzania, and Zimbabwe, maize, along with sorghum and millet, are the most important staple cereals. In fact, an initial substitution of grains in production occurred in these countries in the early part of the century, when the British introduced maize as a staple crop grown on large commercial farms. Sorghum and millet, traditional peasant crops, began to decline in importance at that time. Now, maize is the dominant staple grain in these countries. The current increases in cultivation of maize in Kenya and Zimbabwe, and of sorghum in Tanzania, however, appear to be tied, at least in part, to increased export production, as will be analyzed in further detail below.

During the period covered in this study, maize production in Kenya expanded relative to that of sorghum and millet. In Zimbabwe, millet declined relative to expanding maize cultivation. In both countries, maize is an export growth crop.

By contrast, the share of maize in cereal production declined in Tanzania and South Africa. In Tanzania, the share of maize in grain output has declined relative to the growth in production and export of rice and sorghum. In South Africa, wheat as a proportion of cereal production grew substantially, while maize (the primary food grain) contracted. Exports of wheat grew rapidly in South Africa.

For Kenya, Tanzania, Zimbabwe, and South Africa, then, the grains that are expanding in production are also increasing their share in the volume of grain exports. In Kenya and Zimbabwe, the official government policy is that maize is exported in years when production exceeds domestic consumption needs. This does not appear to be true with respect to the increasing exports of rice from Tanzania and wheat from South Africa. In Table XXIX, we draw a comparison between the increases in production and export of these grains. It should be noted, however, that, in some cases, grain exports overall have declined, so that the larger shares of export trade do not correspond to increasing volume. These instances will be discussed on a case-by-case basis.

The composition of grain imports has also changed in

relation to production and export patterns. To make up for the decline in maize production in Tanzania and South Africa, for example, the volume of maize imports is increasing in relation to wheat. Rice imports have also risen dramatically in relation to wheat in Tanzania and Zimbabwe, apparently in response to changing urban middle sector consumption patterns (see Table XXX).

The volume of food imports, as well as the net grain trade deficit, has grown substantially in Ethiopia, Kenya, Sudan, and Tanzania. South Africa and Zimbabwe, both net grain exporters, have increased the volume of grain exports and their net grain trade surpluses. Dependence on imported food is particularly severe in Ethiopia, Kenya, and Tanzania. Kenya, a net grain exporting country in the 1960s, is now heavily dependent on imports. The change in the values of net grain trade for each country is provided in Table XXXI.

For each of these countries, it is evident that the drought of the 1980s had a catastrophic impact on their net grain trade positions. The other major periods of decline occurred in the early 1970s for Tanzania and in the mid-1970s for Ethiopia. Both Zimbabwe and South Africa, whose trade balances improved dramatically in the 1970s, suffered serious erosion of those surpluses, even though they still remained positive.

In-depth case studies of each of these countries are clearly warranted. It is important, however, to highlight the most salient features that characterize the trends in their food production systems. It is to this task that we now turn.

COUNTRY ANALYSES

Ethiopia

With respect to Ethiopia, the crisis of food production, created in large part by the civil war and years of drought, is not related to a shift from the production of the major food grains to commercial grains for urban consumption, industrial uses, or export. Five grains (wheat, maize, barley, sorghum, and millet) share roughly equal portions of the total grain land, with only minor substitutions having occurred in the 25-year period.

Instead, the impact of the war and drought is reflected in a consistent decline in agricultural production resulting from a drop in both cereal acreage and total cultivated area. The area cultivated in cereals declined at the rate of 0.8% per year, as did the total harvested cropland. Land dedicated to cereal cultivation, which covered an average of 72% of total cropland from 1961 to 1986, declined absolutely from 5.56 million hectares in 1961–1965 to 4.7 million in 1976–1980.

Wheat decreased its share of the land from 16% to 13.6%, while maize increased its share from 14% to 16.5%. Given higher maize yields relative to other grains, maize production increased from 17.6% of total grains in 1961–1965 to 24.7% of the total in 1981–1985. Domestic maize consumption registered a corresponding increase, growing from 15% to 18% of per capita caloric intake between 1961–1965 and 1975–1977 (CIMMYT 1984.) Sorghum acreage has remained constant at almost 19% of the land, barley at 18%, and millet at 5%.

In Table XXXII, we present a comparison of the average area, yields, and production of the major grains for the 25-year period. The loss of acreage in cereal production was made up for in part by increases in productivity, with yields averaging a 1.7% rate of growth and total cereal production growing from 4.1 million tons in 1961–1965 to 5.4 million in 1981–1985. Ethiopia was substantially self-sufficient in foods through the mid-1970s, when grain imports still represented only 1.2% of domestic production. (Grain exports have historically been virtually nonexistent.) Grain imports, made up almost entirely of wheat, tripled to 4.5% of production in 1976–1980 and rose further, to 6.5%, in 1981–1985—still low by international standards; maize imports, while small, have been growing at 22% annually, while rice fell from 17% to 3% of total imports during the quarter-century.

Neither cereal production nor supply, however, has grown as fast as has the population, with the result that per capita production declined by 1.3% annually; and per capita supply, by almost 1% per year.

Sudan

In Sudan, cereal cultivation has averaged over 70% of total cropland since 1961. The area in cereals has expanded at approximately the same rate as has the total harvested area, at 5% per year. Sorghum and millet are the traditional cereal staples of the country, covering an average of 68% and 27% of the total grain land respectively.

One of the most striking features of cereal production in Sudan during this period is the substantial expansion in the area harvested, coupled with the dramatic decline in yields for all cereals. No other country in our study has undergone a comparable drop in yields (see Table XXXIII for a demonstration of the severity of this problem). While cereal area grew at an average rate of 5.2% per year, yields declined by 2.3%.

The substitution of grains in production occurred primarily with respect to an expansion in wheat production for middle and upper income consumption, at the expense of sorghum. This trend took place between 1961 and 1980: Wheat expanded from 1% of the cereal acreage to cover 6%, while sorghum contracted from 71% to 62% of the area. Wheat is cultivated on mechanized farms with heavily subsidized irrigation and other inputs, primarily through the government-sponsored Gezira scheme. As a result, wheat as a proportion of per capita caloric intake rose from 9% to 15% between 1961–1965 and 1979–1981, although the pattern of consumption was highly biased toward urban areas (CIMMYT 1985).

Wheat cultivation relative to sorghum declined somewhat in the 1980s, however. A more detailed case study would need to review whether the drought or changes in government policy influenced this trend. The relative decline of wheat cultivation in the 1980s, however, was compensated by a dramatic rise in wheat imports. Since the 1960s, wheat has constituted over 95% of grain imports. Between 1961 and 1980, imports ranged between 6.3% and 10% of total domestic cereal production. In 1981–1985, however, wheat imports averaged 18.7% of cereal production, double what they had been in the prior 20-year period. At the same time, expanding sorghum production was destined, in part, for increased exports. Grain exports, made up entirely of sorghum, grew by two and a half times between 1971–1975 and 1981–1985, from 69,000 metric tons to 178,000.

South Africa

In South Africa, the substitution of grains in production is taking place with respect to increasing wheat production for urban consumption and export, and declining production of maize, the primary food grain for most of the population. Oats for animal feed have also increased by 50% as a share of cultivated grain land (from 4% to 6% of the land), while sorghum, a food grain, has declined by 20%. The relative drop in maize production has been compensated, in part, by rising maize imports. Traditionally a grain-exporting country, South Africa's trade balance was seriously hurt by the drought of the 1980s. While its grain exports remained steady between 1976–1980 and 1981–1985, the volume of grain imports rose eightfold, from 151,355 metric tons in the first period to 1.3 million in the latter.

In Table XXXIV, we show the major trends during the 25-year period in average area, yields, and production of the major grains. The increasing importance of wheat can be seen; area, yields, and production have all been growing at much faster rates than those of maize.

Kenya

Cultivation of maize, the most important cereal staple in Kenya, covered an average of 76% of the land in cereals and 48% of all cropland in the period 1961–1986. Maize was 58% of the average daily caloric intake of the population in 1980 (Ames and Wojtkowski 1987/1988:209). Official government policy aims at self-sufficiency in maize production. Sorghum and millet, also important staples in some regions, averaged, respectively, 11% and 4% of the cultivated acreage in cereals for the 25-year period. Wheat covered 7% of the area (see Table XXXV).

Agricultural production in Kenya is carried out on small-scale semisubsistence farms, on the one hand, and large-scale commercial operations on the other. Semisubsistence farmers generally produce staple food crops (including cereals, root crops such as cassava, and food bananas) on small plots and supplement these with varying amounts of cash crops. While a majority of maize is grown on these small-scale farms, the large-scale farms also grow maize commercially (Temu 1984:19). These commercial farms also grow a majority of Kenya's export crops, which include coffee, tea, sugarcane, maize, wheat, sisal, and pyrethrum.

Kenya provides an example of how government development and marketing policies may be used to stimulate the agricultural production of smallholders. Government efforts to improve the surplus of small producers began following independence in 1963. Land resettlement of smallholders on formerly European-owned estates continued through the 1960s and 1970s. Out of an estimated farm area of 6.2 million hectares in 1979, approximately two-thirds was distributed among small producers holding plots averaging less than 2 hectares (Jabara 1985:613).

The government also encouraged the formation of agricultural cooperatives to promote production of cash crops and participation in national and export markets: Cash crops included staple grains (primarily maize) as well as other food crops such as coffee, pyrethrum, sugarcane, cotton, milk, and cashew nuts. The National Cereals and Produce Board is the government marketing authority that intervenes in the marketing and pricing of maize and other cereals. Its official purpose is to ensure the availability of basic grains for domestic consumption and the stability of producer prices. Maize and other food crops, however, are also marketed outside of official channels.

An analysis of changes in prices between 1972–1973 and 1982–1983 shows that producer prices generally increased faster than did agricultural input prices for staple cereals, export crops, and industrial crops. Increased production of maize, as well as marketing of surplus production, is attributed to the government's pricing policy for agricultural commodities (Jabara 1985:618). The introduction of short-season hybrid maize, which could be adapted to smallholder cultivation, in the 1960s also contributed to increased maize production in Kenya (Bothmani 1984/1985:152).

By contrast, the government's involvement in the large-scale Perkerra Irrigation Scheme in the Baringo District of Kenya provides an example of how its efforts undermined food self-sufficiency in that region. Promoted in the 1950s as the solution to the region's grain problems, the irrigation scheme failed to achieve expected returns but did increase local maize production. Food production was abandoned, however, in 1963, in favor of growing onions and chiles for export. The shift from domestic market to export production was accompanied by local resistance and price increases in local grains of 300% for maize and 380% for finger millet between 1972 and 1981 (Little and Horowitz 1987:256).

It appears, however, that the major thrust of the Kenyan government since independence has been the promotion of food self-sufficiency through increased distribution of land to small producers and maintenance of producer prices at levels sufficient to encourage production, particularly of maize. Thus, between 1961–1965 and 1981–1985, maize acreage expanded from 75% to 79% of the cultivated cereal land. By contrast, sorghum acreage dropped from 11% to 8% and that of millet from 5.2% to 3.3% (Table XXVIII). Sorghum and millet declined both in area and in yields. Since sorghum and millet are also food grains produced by semisubsistence farmers, it is unclear whether these producers were able to shift to maize, a higher yielding grain, or whether they were displaced. This is an important area for further research.

With only 17% of the land receiving sufficient rainfall for agricultural production, however, a major obstacle for food self-sufficiency is in the overall low growth in output of cereal crops. The slow expansion of cereal production is attributable equally to low growth rates in area and in yields, as is evident in Table XXXV. With only 7% of the land considered to be "first-class" land, and only 15% receiving sufficient rainfall for agricultural production, cultivation is intensive and competition between crops is substantial (Carroll 1987:551). On the other hand, the dry plains areas are extensively used for grazing livestock by subsistence pastoralists.

Thus, the difference between the rapidly growing population, increasing at a rate of 3.9% annually, and the slow growth in food output of 1.5% per year has created a serious gap between domestic production and consumption demand. Per capita cereal production declined by an average of 2.4% per year and per capita cereal supply by 2% each year. Although per capita caloric consumption was found to be above the minimum requirements by one study, it projected a deterioration of the food situation in Kenya by 1990. Another study found that almost 30% of rural preschool children in Kenya suffer chronic undernutrition (Ames and Wojtkowski 1987:210; Kumar 1987:40).

Between 1961–1965 and 1981–1985, the increase in maize production was accompanied by a shift in the composition of grain exports. A comparison of changing grain production and trade indicates that part of the increasing maize output went to the export market and part to the consumption needs of the expanding population. Between 1961–1965 and 1971–1975, when total grain exports were expanding, the share of maize in that total grew from 27% to 57%. Overall grain exports declined between 1971–1975 and 1981–1985, but the share of maize in cereal exports grew to 74.5% in 1976–1980 before dropping to 64% in 1981–1985. Thus, maize exports appear to have increased and decreased according to domestic consumption needs.

As a result of the growing food gap, overall grain imports to Kenya have grown fourfold, from 70,000 metric tons in 1961–1965 to 297,000 in 1981–1985. Grain imports as a proportion of domestic production rose from 3.7% in 1961–1965 to 11.7% in 1981–1985. The composition of grain imports has varied considerably over time, but wheat imports have been consistently the most important. Per capita consumption of wheat has shown a dramatic increase during this period, doubling from 5% to 10% of caloric intake between 1961–1965 and 1979–1981 (CIMMYT 1985).

The Kenyan government, which controls export price policy and domestic grain marketing and pricing, attempts to "get maize prices right" in order to ensure adequate domestic supplies and to export surpluses during years when domestic needs are met. Because this balancing act is not completely successful, substantial quantities of maize are both imported and exported in many years (Temu 1984). The volume of maize imports and exports is erratic, but export volume is regularly much greater than is import volume. The volume of maize exports, for example, was six times greater than that of imports in 1966–1970, 10 times greater in 1971–1975, and 2.5 times greater in 1976–1980. The impact of the drought in the 1980s, however, reversed this equation, with maize imports five times that of exports.

Kenya appears to have done many things right in terms of supporting small-scale producers, providing price supports for the most important staple grain, and promoting food self-sufficiency. Yet, it is one of the few countries that has made the transition from net grain exporter to food importer in the 25-year period reviewed here. Its grain trade balance dropped from U.S. $3.7 million in 1961–1965 to –$3.4 million in 1976–1980 and –$23.9 million in 1981–1985. Clearly, the bulk of the decline occurred during the drought years of the 1980s and may be attributed to that factor. The low growth in yields coupled with a high population growth rate are also contributing factors. While the decline in net grain trade was relatively small between 1961–1965 and 1976–1980, compared to that of other countries in this study, it is not clear from this review what may be the complete explanation for this decline. It is probable, however, that without official efforts to support food self-sufficiency, the current trade deficit would have been much more severe.

Tanzania

Cereal production covers approximately 50% of the 4.3 million hectares of cropland in Tanzania. Unlike the situation in Kenya, the rapid increase in cereal production in Tanzania, averaging 5.1% per year, has significantly outpaced the annual population growth of 3.3%. Consequently, annual per capita production increases have averaged 1.9%, and those of per capita cereal supply, 1.7%. Of the countries included in this study, Tanzania's growth rate in cereal production was exceeded only by that of Venezuela.

In Table XXXVI, we show the growth rates of average area, yields, and production of the most important grains over the 25-year period. The production of maize, the most important staple, has grown rapidly, at a rate of 5% per year. Yet, rice and sorghum output for export has expanded even more rapidly, such that their share of cultivated area and production has increased relative to that of maize. Maize decreased its share of cultivated area from 66% to 51% of the total, and dropped from 62% to 55% of cereal production. Sorghum expanded its share of the area from 13% to 24%, and that of production from 14% to 20%. Rice grew from 7% to 11% of the area, and from 11% to 14% of production (see Table XXVIII). Tanzania's rate of growth of rice output was the fourth highest of any country in the study. The cultivation of millet varied throughout the 25-year period, but its growth rate was slower than that of other cereals and its share of the harvested area generally declined.

Even though maize output has grown significantly, imports have skyrocketed, both in their total volume (from 27,407 metric tons in 1961–1965 to 131,298 in 1981–1985) and as a percentage of overall grain imports (from 31% to 49%). This is the apparent result of expanding production of export grains rather than food grains.

Zimbabwe

The production of maize, the primary staple cereal in Zimbabwe, is growing at 4.2% per year, with acreage expanding at 2.4%, and yields at 1.8% per year (see Table XXXVII). The share of maize in cultivated cereal land rose from 60% to 73% between 1961–1965 and 1981–1985; and with yields considerably higher than those of sorghum and millet, the country's other principal cereals, the share of maize in overall cereal production grew from 73% to 82% in the same period. Domestic consumption of maize also rose during this period. In 1961–1965, it averaged 45% of the total calories in the diet of the population; by 1975–1977, this figure had risen to 55% (CIMMYT 1984).

Maize exports represent the overwhelming bulk, as well as a growing proportion, of Zimbabwe's grain exports: 127,000 metric tons or 77% of the grain exports in 1961–1965 and 249,000 tons or 99% of the total in 1966–1970. Maize exports reached a peak of 435,000 tons in 1971–1975, declining to 303,000 in 1976–1980. Increased demand for domestic consumption during the drought years of the 1980s caused maize exports to decline further to 250,000 tons in 1981–1985, but this may be a temporary trend.

Zimbabwe had virtually achieved its official goal of food self-sufficiency, based on maize, by the late 1970s and had become one of Africa's leading grain exporting countries. Grain imports had declined from 96,000 metric tons in 1961–1965 to 39,000 in 1976–1980, the latter figure representing less than 2% of domestic cereal production. The country's net grain trade balance improved dramatically between 1961 and 1980: It equaled U.S. $1 million in 1961–1965, $29.8 million in 1971–1975, and $24.8 million in 1976–1980. Major increases in grain imports and a decline in exports during the drought years of the 1980s reduced the grain trade surplus to $15 million in 1981–1985 (see Table XXXI).

Wheat is also a growth crop in Zimbabwe. While its share of cereal acreage is still minimal (1.6% in 1981–1985), production grew from virtually nothing in 1961–1965 to 8.7% of total cereal production in 1976–1980, dropping somewhat to 6.8% in 1981–1985. Grown on large-scale mechanized farms for commercial purposes, wheat's yields of 3.8 tons/ha are significantly greater than those of maize; and yields grew at 5.5% per year, three times faster than those of maize. As a result, the overall growth rate of wheat production was 24% per year, the fastest of those for all countries in the study. Per capita consumption of wheat rose from 8% of caloric intake in 1961–1965 to 14% in 1979–1981 (CIMMYT 1985). Leaving aside the crisis years of the 1980s, wheat imports declined substantially in absolute terms between 1961 and 1980, as the country became largely self-sufficient in wheat.

Wheat production began in the 1960s with major

investments in irrigation on plantations, owned by transnational corporations, in the southeastern lowlands. It was stimulated by the introduction of high wheat prices by the government after 1965. By 1971, the country produced 75% of its requirements. And in the mid-1970s, continued high wheat prices led to the expansion of irrigation for wheat production in the highlands of Mashonaland. By the end of that decade, this region produced two-thirds of the wheat in the country (Shopo 1987:52).

The case of Zimbabwe offers some interesting contradictions for our study. On the one hand, it is among the few developing countries that achieved self-sufficiency in food and became a net grain exporter. On the other, it represents, along with Kenya and Tanzania, perhaps the most advanced example of the substitution of grains in production. Substitution of maize for sorghum and millet began in the 1920s and 1930s. Varieties of sorghum and millet had been the staple subsistence crops of the indigenous population since the sixteenth century.

Maize, first grown on the white commercial farms, covered a substantial portion of those farms by the 1930s. A uniform system of producer prices was established in 1934 under the Maize Control Act in order to ensure inexpensive supplies of maize for food as well as to provide feed for livestock. The main cash crops for export, however, were tobacco and cotton, with maize grown as a complementary food crop. Its expansion thus depended on the profitability of tobacco and cotton. When tobacco prices began falling from the 1950s on, maize increasingly became the substitute crop (Shopo 1987:33–49). Thus, Zimbabwe's main food crop, produced on large-scale commercial farms, became one of its most important export crops. Since the 1950s, virtually all maize is marketed through the Grain Marketing Board (GMB).

Maize production expanded, and yields were higher than those of sorghum and millet, because the farms of white settlers were located in the areas of the best soil and rainfall. For commercial farming purposes, the country is divided into five agroecological regions, based largely on rainfall. Conditions are increasingly marginal for farming from Natural Region I to V (Zinyama 1986:109). Commercial farms cover three-fourths of the land in the two best regions, while the communal areas are situated on three-quarters of the land in the two worst regions (Billing 1985).

In the last 20 years, maize cultivation in the communal areas has expanded very rapidly, even though a midseason drought and poor soils make them relatively unsuited for maize production. As a result, yields of maize in these areas are one-sixth as great as those in the commercial areas, but they still may be higher than those of sorghum and millet.[26] Despite this disadvantage, an increasing proportion of the maize bought by the GMB comes from the communal areas, a proportion that reached the unusual high of 40% in 1984 (Billing 1985:120–124).

Today, the structure of agriculture still carries the legacy of the colonial period, with production divided into four sectors: large-scale white commercial farms producing 90% of the marketable crops, including maize, and the major export crops, tobacco and cotton; small-scale farms, formerly the African Purchase Areas, producing a combination of food and cash crops; the communal areas, formerly the Tribal Trust Lands; and the Resettlement Areas, formerly commercial farmland. The latter two sectors are oriented primarily toward subsistence production of sorghum, millet, and maize, with the production of maize and cotton for market on the increase.

Thus, commercial maize production and, since the 1960s, wheat production have continued to expand while the traditional food grains of the indigenous population have declined. A summary of the average area, yields, and output of these grains, as well as their growth rates, is provided in Table XXXVII.

Most notable is the wide variation in yields of these crops, reflecting major differences in the conditions under which they are grown: wheat in irrigated conditions; the majority of maize in rainfed areas; and sorghum and millet in poor, dry regions. As a result, sorghum and millets (*mhunga, rapoko*) declined in importance. Yields of both crops had a 25-year average of only 500 kg/ha, one-third that of maize, and they declined at an annual rate of 0.8% and 1.6%, respectively. The area cultivated in millet also declined, at a rate of 2.3% per year, with the result that its share decreased from 32% to 14% of the land in cereals. Overall millet output declined from 21% of the total to 6%. While sorghum acreage increased during the period, yields declined more rapidly, with the result that sorghum production declined in importance from 5% to 4% of cereal output (Billing 1985:20).

Since independence in 1980, the black majority government has begun to reverse some of the most glaring inequalities inherited from the colonial administration, land redistribution being the most pressing. The government has proceeded cautiously, however, given the dependence of the country's economy on the commercial farm sector and a strong constitutional prohibition against compulsory expropriation of land. Three years of drought (1981–1984), coupled with the international recession and the lack of available foreign assistance, also hindered progress (Zinyama 1986:108).

The number of government loans to producers in the communal areas and resettlement program lands has grown from zero in 1978–1979 to 65,000 in 1983–1984, while the number of loans to large-scale farmers has been halved. This correponds to a dramatic change in the amount of maize reaching the government marketing board from each sector: Deliveries from the large-scale sector represented 96.5% of the total in 1974/75, 92.5% in 1979/80, but only 61.7% in 1984/85. Those from the small-scale commercial and communal sectors rose proportionately from 3.5% in 1974/75 to 7.5% in 1979/80 and 38.3% in 1984/85 (Zinyama 1986:112).

The case of Zimbabwe offers a clear example of how the move toward food self-sufficiency in itself did not represent an improvement in rural welfare, given the structural constraints in the agrarian sector. Large-scale commercial food production supplanted traditional peasant agriculture for decades until the country underwent a revolution to remove white minority rule. The new government appears to be moving in the direction of changing these inequalities among rural producers through the land resettlement program, loans to small producers, the establishment of agricultural cooperatives, and other measures. It is clearly too early to assess the long-term impacts of these changes.

7

The Substitution of Grains in Asia

REGIONAL OVERVIEW

The patterns of substitution in grain production and trade in Asia vary according to three distinct subregions: southern Asia (Bangladesh and India), southeastern Asia (Indonesia, the Philippines, and Thailand), and China. In southern Asia, wheat cultivation is displacing traditional staples: rice in Bangladesh and sorghum and millet in India. Wheat imports are also replacing rice imports in Bangladesh, while the composition of grain imports to India has remained relatively unchanged. In southeastern Asia, the substitution in grain cultivation is taking place between maize and rice, but the trends are contradictory. Rice is displacing maize in Indonesia and the Philippines, but the opposite is occurring in Thailand. China is a world unto itself, and the changes in cereal production are more complex, involving increases and decreases in several crops. These patterns are presented in Table XXXVIII.

The Asian countries included in this study share some common tendencies with respect to their changing grain trade. First, rice imports are declining in all countries but China and Thailand, both of which are rice-exporting countries. The increases in output of rice are due to the concerted efforts of governments to achieve self-sufficiency in food production through government-sponsored irrigation projects, the introduction of high yielding varieties, and the increased use of fertilizer, among other strategies.

A second phenomenon, common to Bangladesh, the Philippines, and China, is that the cereal that is expanding in area of cultivation is also the cereal that is consuming an ever larger portion of grain imports to those countries. A comparison of tables XXXIX and XL makes this pattern evident. Bangladesh has expanded wheat cultivation by 5% of total area, and wheat imports have increased by 40%. Maize cultivation has expanded by 11% of the total grain area in the Philippines; maize imports have grown from zero to 25% of the total grain imports at the same time. The increase in wheat and decrease in barley cultivation in China is coupled with rising wheat imports and declining barley imports to that country.

India and Thailand follow a different pattern. Their expanded wheat production is in part oriented toward the export market. Notably, in Indonesia, where wheat production has not been expanding, dependency on wheat imports is significantly greater than in any of the other countries. Wheat constituted 10% of the imports in 1961–1965 and 76% in 1981–1985.

A third common feature of the Asian countries reviewed here is their serious efforts to move toward food self-sufficiency in the last 25 years. While all but Thailand are still net grain importers, the volume of imports compared to exports has declined significantly in each. Nonetheless, the value of net grain trade has continued to deteriorate for each country but Thailand and India, as is indicated in Table XL.

A brief review of each country identifies the major trends.

COUNTRY ANALYSES

Bangladesh

Bangladesh is one of the most impoverished and food import dependent countries in the world, although it has made major and continuing efforts to improve its food self-sufficiency. In Table XLI, we show the trends in area, yields, and production of the major grains over the 25-year period reviewed here. Despite positive rates of growth, the overall situation deteriorated further as population growth surpassed cereal production. Per capita grain production decreased by 0.5% per year; per capita supply, by 0.4%. Population pressure on the land is severe, and landlessness is on the rise.

Rice represents an average of 97% of grain cultivation. Efforts to increase yields through the spread of high yielding varieties and use of chemical inputs have not been as widespread or had the success rate of efforts in other Asian countries. Rice yields averaged 1.8 kg/ha and grew at 1.3% per year.[27]

Wheat cultivation was introduced in this period as an attempt to diversify agriculture and provide a lower cost cereal for the poorest people in Bangladesh. It is considered to be inferior to any type of rice but has grown to represent 5% of total grain cultivation. Most of the added wheat area came from land, formerly planted in rice, that had been abandoned. Thus, areas that had insufficient water for dry-season rice but did have some moisture or irrigation from pumps could be converted to wheat cultivation. The availability of winter wheat has also helped to ease seasonal shortages. Per capita wheat consumption grew from 4% of total caloric intake in 1961–1965 to 10% in 1979–1981, owing in part to production increases and in part to the availability of wheat as international food aid.

Despite these efforts toward food self-sufficiency, the volume of grain imports doubled between 1961–1965 and 1981–1985, and Bangladesh's grain deficit bill quadrupled. While rice imports as a percentage of total imports dropped by over one-half, from 33% to 15%, wheat imports grew from 44% to 85% of the total (see Table XXXIX).

India

Agricultural production in India is highly diversified compared to that of many Asian countries. Traditional cereal staples include rice, several varieties of sorghum and millet, and pulses such as chick-peas and pigeon peas, which are intercropped with sorghum and millet. During the past 25 years, the area in rice cultivation changed very little and covered an average of 38% of the land in cereal cultivation; millet averaged 20% and sorghum 17%. Wheat covered an average of 18% of the area during the same time period (Table XLII).

The majority of India, however, is "sorghum and millet country." That is, 80% of the land is in the semiarid tropics. Without irrigation facilities, inadequate rainfall limits the areas of growth for wheat and rice. By contrast, drought resistant sorghum and millet are well adapted to these conditions, and 95% of the cultivation of these crops is done in rainfed areas without access to irrigation (Mahapatra et al. 1986:6–8).

The area dedicated to sorghum cultivation in India constitutes 37% of the world area in sorghum, significantly more than India's 28% share of world rice cultivation. Low yields, however, reduce India's shares in world production of sorghum and rice to 17.2% and 19.7%, respectively.

Sorghum and millet are traditional poor people's crops, the overwhelming proportion of which are grown for home consumption. Eighty-five percent of production is concentrated in the northern states of Maharashtra, Madhya Pradesh, Andhra Pradesh, and Karnataka. Recent marketing studies have shown that an average of 75% of sorghum production is consumed by producers, with approximately 51% used for home consumption, 20% used as wage payments, and 4% retained for seed. The exceptions to the rule are large farmers in the vicinity of markets, who sell a substantial proportion of their harvest (von Oppen and Rao 1982:660–666).

In addition to use of sorghum grain for direct human consumption, sorghum straw is the main source of animal feed in the regions where it is grown. For this reason, farmers have resisted changing to dwarf varieties, even though this decision means a continuation of low yields (Mahapatra *et al.* 1986:7).

Where soils permit, sorghum (including *jowar* and *bajra*) and millet are traditionally intercropped with pulses. This practice covers 35% to 73% of gross cropped area in regions where it is feasible, and it is practiced much more extensively by small farmers than by larger ones. While intercropping is criticized as a "backward practice" that lowers yields, it allows for higher gross returns and a more even utilization of labor when compared to single cropping (Spitz 1987:64–66).

This traditional production system has been eroded with the expansion of capital-intensive, monocrop, irrigated cultivation of rice, and especially wheat, in the last two decades. Under the impact of the green revolution beginning in the mid-1960s, wheat became the major growth crop in India. With the rapid expansion of irrigation, wheat grew from 14% of the cultivated grain area in 1961–1965 to 22% in 1981–1985. Irrigated land grew at a rate of 2.3% between 1960 and 1980 and covered 24% of the crop area by 1980. By the late 1970s, 35% of the rice crop was irrigated (Herdt *et al.* 1985:98). While 60% of wheat is grown under irrigated conditions, less than 5% of sorghum and millet cropland is irrigated, even though sorghum and millet yields increase significantly with irrigation (Spitz 1987:61).

At 3.6% per year, the growth rate of wheat yields was

substantially higher than that of any other grain: twice that of rice (1.7% per year); two and a half times the rate of sorghum (1.4%); and over three times that of millet (0.9%). As a result, the share of wheat as a proportion of total cereal production rose from 13% in 1961–1965 to 26% in 1981–1985. The share of rice declined from 60% to 54% of the total.

By contrast, the area cultivated in sorghum and millet declined by 0.5% per year. The percentage of cereal area dedicated to sorghum declined from 19.4% to 15.5% in the 25-year period. That of millet decreased from 20% to 16%. A comparison of the average area, yields, and output of grains and their annual growth rates is provided in Table XLII.

The area cultivated in pulses has also declined as a result of the expansion of wheat production, by 22% according to a 1977 study. And the growth rate of yields of pulses was –1.1% for the period from 1967/68 to 1979/80 (Spitz 1987:61).

Per capita wheat consumption in India has increased over the past 25 years, with wheat constituting 19% of the total caloric intake of the population in 1961–1965 and 27% in 1979–1981 (CIMMYT 1985). A substantial portion of the expanded wheat production, however, has been geared toward the export market. Between 1961–1965 and 1976–1980, wheat grew from 12% of the grain export market to 52%. In the same period, rice dropped from 84% to 34%. Grain exports from India underwent a dramatic reversal in the period 1981–1985, with wheat exports falling to 12% of the total and rice composing 86%. The reasons for this change are not entirely clear.

The green revolution in wheat production helped India offset its food deficit bill and, by the 1976–1980 period, reduce the volume of food imports to approximately one-third of what they had been in 1961–1965. But with land and income distribution highly skewed, the majority of the population did not participate in the benefits. The strategy resulted in a widening of disparities among social groups and among regions and created a basis for major social unrest. As a consequence, the government of India particularly addressed the issue of social justice in its fifth and sixth Five Year plans (1974–1979 and 1978–1983). It established integrated rural development programs to reduce inequalities and develop self-reliance among small producers (Sarma 1986:10).

An assessment of these special equity programs eight years after implementation found that they had not had any measurable effect; coverage had been inadequate, implementation ineffective, and efforts to integrate crop production and subsidiary activities programs had failed. "Because the new technology is so far largely confined to irrigated and assured rainfall areas and because it requires good infrastructure development to facilitate input distribution and output marketing, interregional disparities have been accentuated in the post–green revolution period" (Sarma 1986:30). Other studies have also found that the new technology depended on the availability of capital to be taken advantage of, and widened disparities in income between small and large farmers while squeezing out marginal and small farmers and increasing landlessness.[28]

Those states where the green revolution was introduced have clearly benefited, mainly Punjabi Suba, Haryana, western Uttar Pradesh, and some areas of Andhra Pradesh, Tamil Nadu, and Maharashtra. But the bulk of the country, the semiarid "sorghum and millet country," has not. The growth of nontraditional commercial and export-oriented wheat production has been at the expense of the poor, largely rural, population, not only because of the increased polarization that it has engendered but the missed opportunities to improve the basic food crops that still, after 20 years of erosion, cover a third of the Indian countryside.

Philippines

In the Philippines, the government began a drive for rice self-sufficiency in the mid-1960s. Modern varieties of rice were introduced, and, thanks in part to the presence of the International Rice Research Institute in that country, they were distributed more extensively than in any other southeastern Asian country (Herdt *et al.* 1985:254).

By far the best-financed and most successful effort of the government was the Masagana 99 program, initiated in 1973 and intended primarily to increase rice production through the widespread adoption of high yielding varieties, combined with subsidized fertilizer and chemical pest control. By 1982, 85% of the land cultivated in rice was sown with high yielding varieties (Gómez 1985:46).

Increased rice production was due entirely to yield increases, which grew at an annual rate of 3.3%. The Philippines achieved basic self-sufficiency in rice by the mid-1970s but resumed substantial imports in the 1980s.

The share of area cultivated in rice, however, has declined relative to that in maize, second most important staple food in the country. But expansion of maize acreage was in response to increasing feed demand, not for direct human consumption. Demand for maize for feed increased twice as fast as maize output in the 1970s (Koppel 1987:165). Maize imports for feed use also rose significantly, from zero in 1961–1965 to 25% of total grain imports in 1981–1985 (from zero to 315,000 metric tons per year).

Maize increased its share of the land dedicated to cereal production from 39% in 1961–1965 to 50% in 1981–1985. The share of land in rice cultivation declined correspondingly, from 61% of the land area to 50% (Table XXXVIII). It is striking that maize cultivation has expanded so rapidly, because its productivity is much lower than that of rice. Although maize cultivation covered 50% of the land by 1981–1985, maize output constituted only 30% of overall cereal production. Rice, grown on the remaining 50% of the cereal land, accounted for 70% of total grain output. In Table XLIII we compare average area, yields, and production of maize and rice for the 25-year period.

Cereal production grew at a rate considerably faster than that of the population— 4% per year versus 2.7% —yielding a net gain in per capita cereal production of 1.3% per year. Nonetheless, grain imports increased in the 25-year period, from an average of 677,000 metric tons in 1961–1965 to 1.28 million tons in 1981–1985.

Thus, despite efforts to achieve self-sufficiency, the volume of grain imports doubled between 1961–1965 and 1981–1985. The value of the net grain trade of the Philippines deteriorated from –$60 million to more than –$200 million in 1981–1985.

Thailand

Historically one of the world's major producers and exporters of rice, a rich agricultural country with a comparative advantage in the production of numerous crops, Thailand is still unable to meet the nutritional needs of its people. While cereal production increased at a rate of 3.2% in the last 25 years (see Table XLIV), ahead of the population increase of 2.6%, per capita cereal supply actually declined by 0.2% per year.

Rice constitutes two-thirds of the average urban diet and

three-fourths of the rural diet of Thai people (Trairatvorakul 1984:20). The share of rice in cereal production and overall agricultural production, however, has been declining since 1960. Rice covered an average of 94% of the land in grains in 1961–1965 and 84% in 1981–1985. Its share in cereal production decreased from 93% to 82% in that period. By contrast, maize, destined entirely for animal feed, expanded from 6% of the land to 14%, or at a rate of 7.5% per year (see Table XXXVIII). With yields slightly higher than those of rice (2.2 kg/ha versus 1.9 kg/ha), maize output grew from 7% to 17% of total cereal production. Rice production grew at a rate of 2.5% per year, slower than the population growth rate, while maize production expanded at 8.3% annually. While sorghum is still only a minor crop, it grew at a rate of 8.5% per year (from zero in 1961–1965 to 2.5% of the land in 1981–1985). Maize and sorghum are grown for the domestic feed industry and for export.

The growth in rice, as well as maize, has occurred mainly through the expansion of area rather than yields. This is in large part the result of government policies. Agricultural research has focused almost entirely on improving rice under irrigated conditions. Government-sponsored irrigation has grown at 7.1% per year since 1961 and now covers one-quarter of the total cropland. Thus, the vast majority of crops are still produced in rainfed conditions. In addition, over two-thirds of the irrigated area is located in the central plains region, compared to 16% in the north, 10% in the northeast, and 6% in the south. Moreover, government policies have encouraged monopolies in the production and importation of fertilizers, so that prices are twice the level of those of other Asian countries. Consequently, fertilizer use is extremely low compared to that of other rice-producing countries (Puapanichya and Panaytou 1985:43).

Domestic rice prices are also kept considerably below world levels. As a result, Thai rice producers are penalized. According to one researcher, "Low farm prices for paddy, coupled with an extraordinary high price for fertilizer, have left Thai farmers in a very unfavorable position compared with farmers in neighboring importing countries" (Herdt et al. 1985:252). While farm prices of rice doubled between 1968 and 1979, those of maize more than tripled, so that they almost equaled the price of rice in 1979 (Puapanichya and Panaytou 1985:51).

Other cash and export-oriented crops, particularly cassava and sugarcane, have also expanded more rapidly than has rice.

Cassava is produced almost entirely for the animal feed industry of the European Economic Community. Cane is produced for domestic consumption and for export. The contribution of rice to the value of agricultural production decreased from 44% in 1960 to 33% in 1983; that of maize and sorghum increased from 2% to 5%, sugarcane from 2% to 9%, and cassava from 2% to 7%. A similar shift occurred among agricultural exports. The value of rice exports dropped from 40% of the total in 1960 to 21% in 1982. Cassava contributed only 5% in 1960 and 18% in 1982; cane grew from 2% to 13%, and maize from 6% to 8% during the same period (Isarangkura 1986:3–6).

A comparison of the growth rates of domestic consumption versus exports of these commodities shows that, with the exception of maize, exports have grown at a much more rapid rate, as indicated in Table XLV. The government of Thailand intervenes minimally in the export market, compared to other Asian countries. The equivalent of an export tax is placed on rice, apparently to control the export volume.

This period of important agricultural changes has been accompanied by dramatic increases in landlessness and tenancy. Unlike the experience of other Asian countries, tenancy arrangements have been historically insignificant in Thailand. Between 1962–1963 and 1975–1976, however, tenancy increased from 3.8% to 11.8% of the total landholding. The problem was most severe in the central plains, where tenancy rose from 14.7% to 38.3% of the landholding in the same period. It was the mildest in the northeast, where tenancy accounted for 2.7% of property in 1975–1976. A government study found that the rapid growth in tenancy was due to the loss of land caused by the accumulation of debts (Puapanichya and Panaytou 1985:48–49).

Seasonal interregional labor migration is also significant. Migrant labor demand for four crops alone (sugarcane, pineapple, dry season rice, and tapioca) was estimated at over 350,000 workers in 1981. The major migration routes run from the northeast and north to the central plains, the south, and Bangkok. Almost 80% of migrants from the northeast, according to one study, come from households where rice production is either inadequate to meet family needs or at subsistence level. Most migrants leave for lack of employment opportunities at home and for economic reasons. However, over 60% of migrants to Bangkok do not earn enough to remit any cash back home (Panpiemras and Krusuansombat 1985:321–337).

Increases in unemployment, underemployment, and landlessness exacerbate the already existing income disparities in the country, both among social groups and between one region and another. Income and nutritional disparities are also highly correlated in Thailand, as elsewhere (Trairatvorakul 1984).

According to Thai consumer surveys, food accounts for an average of 50% of domestic expenditures, equaling 100% of those of the lowest income group and decreasing to 13% of the highest. In the northeast and in the Bangkok slums, the most impoverished areas, the percentage of income spent on food averaged 61% and 58%, respectively, in 1982. In the northeast, 52.3% of the households in 1980 were below the poverty line, and 56.7% of the children under five years old suffered from malnutrition. The percentage of children suffering from malnutrition was 50.8 in the northern region, 43.5 in the south, and 36.6 in the central plains (Konjing and Veerakitpanich 1985:165).

Moreover, a 1982 national survey of 1.4 million Thai children found that 34% suffered from first-degree malnutrition, 12% from second-degree malnutrition, and 2% from third-degree malnutrition. It found that dietary intake of infants, preschool- and schoolchildren, and pregnant and lactating mothers was far below the recommended level. Average caloric intake in rural areas was 1,821 calories per day, and in the Bangkok slums 1,504 calories per day (Konjing and Veerakitpanich 1985:165). Another study found that, on the average, 26% of Thai households are below the poverty line and that, based on a requirement of 2,500 calories per day per adult, one-half of urban and rural households are deficient (Trairatvorakul 1984).

Clearly, development policies pursued by the Thai government that favor feed and export-oriented crops over staple food production contribute to these social and economic inequalities, put the food security of the country at risk, and perhaps jeopardize the well-being of a major portion of the population.

Indonesia

Indonesia is one of the few cases in this study[29] where the substitution of grains in production has favored the most important staple cereal. Between 1969 and 1974, Indonesia went from being the world's largest importer of rice to a net exporter. This is due primarily to the concerted efforts of the Indonesian government since the 1960s to achieve self-sufficiency in food production. Overall cereal production has increased at the rapid rate of 4.8% per year since 1961, the third highest of any country's in the study, and the increase is due entirely to rice output. Total rice output grew at 5.2% annually, faster than that of any of the major rice-producing countries considered here (see Table XLVI).

The expansion of rice production, however, has often been at the expense of maize, Indonesia's second most important food grain. Three-fourths of maize production is for direct human consumption. Maize accounts for 10% of all calories and protein consumed by the population, but it is eaten almost entirely in rural producing regions and by low income consumers. And over half of production is marketed, primarily to landless workers and the rural poor. "Corn is the staple foodstuff . . . for 18 million people and is grown by more than 10 million farm households" (Dorosh et al. 1987:19). It plays a particularly crucial role in the regions where it is grown, among low income groups, and for the rural poor during the *paceklik* or "hungry season," before the main rice harvest on Java (Monteverde and Mink 1987:111).

During the period considered in this study, land cultivated in rice, which supplies the majority of the protein and caloric intake of the population, increased from 71% to 78% of the total grain area. Maize underwent a corresponding decline in cultivated area, from 29% to 22% of the total. This represents an absolute decline from 2.9 million to 2.7 million hectares.

Rice yields averaged over twice those of maize and grew at a faster rate. While rice yields averaged 2.7 metric tons/ha, with an annual growth rate of 3.6% for the 25-year period, maize yields were 1.2 metric tons/ha, with a growth rate of 2.8% per year. Thus, rice production grew from 82% to 89% of total grain output, and maize production shrank from 18% to 11%.

In contrast to Thailand, Indonesia has historically been among the world's largest rice importers. Between 1956 and 1964, rice imports grew annually, reaching a peak of 2 million metric tons (Herdt et al. 1985,249). In order to reverse this import dependency, the government initiated a series of policies to increase rice production dramatically. In 1965–1966, the Bimbingan Masal (BIMAS) program was established to provide, on a massive scale, technical assistance, credit, and subsidized inputs to farmers. Modern rice varieties were introduced in

1968.

Beginning in 1969, the first Five Year Plan (Repelita I) set as its goal self-sufficiency in rice production. In the early 1970s, intensified support services were provided through "village units," blocks of agricultural areas between 600 and 1,000 hectares in size, which were the recipients of credit, subsidized fertilizer, extension services, and government purchases of rice. In 1979, the Intensifikasi Khusus (INSUS) program was established, which provided for a more collectivized approach to production. Groups of up to 50 farmers were formed for purposes of making collective decisions for land preparation, planting, spraying, harvesting, credit approval, and loan repayment (Nestel 1985).

Because of the shortage and uneven distribution of land, most of the growth in production had to come from intensified use. Over 60% of the farms in Indonesia are less than 1 hectare and 30% are less than 0.25 hectare; most cultivated land is located on the islands of Java and Bali (Nestel 1985). Although the cultivated area in the country expanded by 13.3% between 1963 and 1973, little or none of the increase took place on Java. Intensification has come about through heavy government subsidies for fertilizer—over half a billion dollars in 1985 (Timmer 1987:276)—and through heavy investments in irrigation. For example, between 1963 and 1973, there was an 18% increase in the total irrigated area, with the major part of the increase on Sumatra, Kalimantan, and Sulawesi (World Bank 1980:29).

The BIMAS and INSUS programs, largely confined to irrigated areas, covered approximately one-quarter of Indonesia's wetland rice land by 1980. Approximately 53% of the total land cultivated in rice is irrigated wetland. Government subsidies of inputs led to a fivefold increase in the use of modern seed varieties, a threefold increase in fertilizer use, and a substantial rise in the use of insecticides. A minimum price floor for rice has also been maintained to ensure production incentives (Nestel 1985).

As a result of these policies, advances in production allowed Indonesia to achieve rice self-sufficiency by the end of Repelita II in the late 1970s. The great majority of increased output was due to improved yields, which increased at between 5% and 10% per year in the 1970s.

Critics of the program, however, have noted that its impact on producers and consumers was highly uneven. While the government maintained consumer prices for rice at low levels, costs for other foodstuffs, including maize, cassava, sweet potatoes, soybeans, and peanuts, as well as for nonfood consumer items, continued to rise. Consumption of other foodstuffs declined, as did the total per capita dry-weight intake (Timmer 1981:40).

Repelita III (1978–1983) shifted focus to *palawija*, or secondary crops, because, according to some accounts, self-sufficiency in rice had been achieved. According to others, it was recognized that increases in rice production began to decline in the mid-1970s, that rice could not keep up with domestic demand, and that maize and cassava provided the potential to avoid food import dependency (Timmer 1987:19).

Two crops per year can be grown on over two-thirds of the irrigated land in Indonesia. The most important *palawija* crops include maize, cassava (*gaplek*), sweet potatoes, soybeans, groundnuts, and mung beans, grown primarily for domestic consumption. Indonesian production of cassava equals 10% of world production and supplies 8% of the national caloric intake. Direct human consumption of cassava is widespread, both in urban and rural areas, but particularly among low income households. Domestic soybean production is also for direct consumption, while an equal amount is imported for animal feed (Nestel 1985).

Maize production also benefited from some of the policies established to increase rice production. Increase in yields has occurred because of the growing use of subsidized fertilizer. Use of hybrid and improved open-pollinated varieties has also begun to make an impact. Most of the maize, however, is still grown on land that cannot be irrigated. On the demand side, the fastest-growing component is maize to be used in the livestock feed industry. Should incomes rise in the country, it is to be expected that there will be an increase in meat consumption because per capita consumption in 1980 was less than 4 kilograms per year (Mink 1987:143). This would be likely to increase demand for maize as a feed. Although the country has been a net exporter, there were some prospects that Indonesia would become an importer of maize in the late 1980s (Dorosh *et al.* 1987:23). This would be even more likely if the government were to remove the subsidies on fertilizer.

The impact of policies to improve self-sufficiency in food in Indonesia are impressive. The country is one of the few that has invested substantially in ways that encourage the production of basic staples. One result is that per capita availability of rice increased from 90.6 kilograms per year in 1960–1967 to over 140 in 1985. The average per capita daily intake of calories increased from 1,953 in 1968–1970 to 2,506 in 1979–1980. The country experienced substantial increases in employment, a rise in real living standards, and a decline in the number of households with low levels of per capita consumption. The rapid rise in agricultural output and incomes during the 1970s was a singularly important influence on the improving situation in Indonesia (World Bank 1980:95).

The contrast between Indonesia and Nigeria—both countries that experienced an oil boom—is especially telling. Nigeria borrowed heavily and resisted any devaluation of its currency during the 1970s. It increased public expenditures in primary education, transport, and construction. In contrast, Indonesia kept its real exchange rate steady and invested in physical infrastructure, education, capital-intensive industry, and agricultural development. While government policies resulted in an average annual decline of 7.9% in agriculture in Nigeria from 1973 to 1983, Indonesia's agriculture grew 3.1% per year during the same period (World Bank 1986:72).

Indonesia's extremely positive results have to be tempered somewhat. The 40% of the population with the lowest income levels still falls below the FAO recommended level of daily caloric consumption. While technological innovations in agriculture have greatly increased food production as well as the incomes of producers, they have not generated increased employment. On the island of Java, where the transformation in agriculture has been the greatest, agricultural employment grew at the rate of 1% annually in the 1970s, as opposed to 1.4% in the 1960s. In some instances, the technological innovations have displaced labor, and the real wages of landless laborers and marginal farmers have not increased. The same World Bank study (1980:98) that noted the improvement in the country cautioned that "careful attention is required to the impact of agricultural growth on the structure of landholdings and tenure conditions and the avoidance of undesirable increases in the concentration of wealth and income in the agricultural sector."

Because of Indonesia's successful attempt at achieving self-sufficiency, further analysis of its food system is warranted. It is important to determine whether the poorest sectors of the population have benefited from the agricultural revolution to the same extent as other, higher income groups have done. And it will be interesting to see whether, having substantially improved the food self-sufficiency and food security situation, the country will retreat from the policies that brought it success.

China

China's most striking achievement in agricultural production is the consistent improvement in yields of all grains over the past 25 years.[30] These data have to be interpreted with some caution, however, because the beginning point corresponds to the Great Leap Forward period (1958–1960) when bad weather, bad planning, and technical mismanagement led to massive famines (Walker 1984:129). In 1961, China became a net importer of food for the first time since the early 1950s. Nevertheless, while the total area allocated to cereal production has remained virtually unchanged, overall grain yields grew at an annual average of 4.7%, the highest sustained rate of increase of any major grain-producing country. This performance contributed significantly to China's improved capacity to move toward food self-sufficiency. With little variation in area, total grain production also grew at 4.7% per year, almost two and a half times the rate of population growth (1.9%). Thus, per capita cereal supply (including net foreign trade) also rose at a rate of 2.7% per year in this period.

Despite these efforts, China is still heavily dependent on grain imports, which doubled in volume between 1961–1965 and 1981–1985. While the volume of China's grain exports also doubled during this time, the net value of its grain trade declined at an average of 1.7% per year.

The growth of output of basic staples in China over the past 25 years has been spectacular. A comparison of China with 24 other countries, in Asia, Africa, and Latin America, shows that it ranks fourth in terms of its annual average growth rate of total cereal production. It ranks first, however, in the rate of growth of grain yields. In fact, improvements in yields account for virtually all of the increases in production over the 25 years.

This pattern of growth in productivity is remarkably consistent among each of the individual grains. In addition to rice, wheat and maize are major staple crops in China. For the 25-year period under review, these three crops accounted for 83% of the land dedicated to cereals: Rice accounted for an average of 35% of the cultivated grain area; wheat, 29%; and maize, 19%. In all three cases, the significant expansion in output occurred primarily as a result of yield increases, as can be seen in Table XLVII.

However, there have been some notable changes in the composition of grain production in China in this period. The area dedicated to rice, wheat, and maize has increased relative to overall grain area, while sorghum, millet, barley, and oats have undergone a corresponding decline (see Table XLVII). Although the change for each crop is relatively small, when taken together these changes account for a shift in the use of almost 15% of the land dedicated to cereals. The pattern of substitution in grain production is more clearly presented in Table XLVIII.

With the exception of oat production, which in any case is almost insignificant, the shifts in cultivated area are not explained by the yield data. Yields of sorghum, millet, and barley also increased significantly during the period in question. The reason for the decline in area sown in coarse grains reflects the growing availability of the preferred rice and wheat. By 1982, it was reported that "even an average peasant family consumed 75 percent of its grain as milled rice or wheat flour, a ratio available only with privileged urban cadre rations a few years earlier" (Smil 1985:251).

The rate of growth in cereal production has varied somewhat over time. The highest growth rate took place throughout the 1960s, when increase in output averaged 6% per year. This average declined to 4.8% between 1970 and 1975, and to 3.8% during 1976–1980. In the 1981–1985 period, it climbed back to 4.6%.[31] The very large increases in grain production have often caused difficulty because storage systems are inadequate to take full advantage of bumper harvests.

Although there was a slight drop in the rate of growth of production during 1976–1980, the inclusion of net grain trade allows us to affirm that the actual per capita grain supply was considerably greater during this period. Food balance sheets indicate that per capita consumption in 1977 reached the levels of the period between 1956 and 1958 "and was just marginally higher than average food availability during the years immediately preceding the start of the Sino-Japanese War in 1937" (Smil 1985:248).

The major exception to the positive trends in availability of basic foodstuffs is soybean production. China's high point in production of this legume was in 1936 when about 22 kilograms per capita were available. By 1984, production had fallen to only about 9.36 kilograms per person. Because the Chinese had decided to stop importing soybeans, and because about half the soybean crop is used for oil, per capita availability of these high protein legumes was only about 5 kilograms per year (Smil 1985:249).

China's grain trade has shown considerably more variation than has its grain production over the last 25 years. Between 1961 and 1975, China was moving toward self-sufficiency in cereals. The total volume of grain imports dropped from an average of 6 million metric tons per year (1961–1965) to 5 million tons (1966–1975). At the same time, grain exports were increasing, from an average of 1 million tons in 1961–1965 to 2 million tons in 1971–1975.

This trend reversed itself in 1976. Imports more than doubled in the period from 1976 to 1986. They averaged 8.5 million tons between 1976 and 1980, and 11.9 million tons between 1981 and 1986. The volume of grain exports dropped from an average of 2 million tons per year in the early 1970s to 1.3 million tons per year in 1976–1980. The decline in exports was primarily observed in rice, which composed 94% of all exports.

Although the volume of grain exports in the 1980s has returned to its 1971–1975 level, their composition has changed markedly. Maize now constitutes 33% of the volume of grain exports, while rice declined from 96% of all exports in the late 1960s to 65% in the early 1980s. This export strategy probably reflected a decision to facilitate increased domestic rice consumption, in spite of the fact that it has had a negative impact on China's trade balance. The value of maize exports is only 24% of the total; that of rice is 74%. Thus, the substitution of the lower valued maize for rice in the export market means that China is earning relatively less foreign exchange for its exports, even though the volume of exports has increased.

At the same time, grain imports have continued to rise. Over 90% of these are wheat imports. The combined effect of the export of lower valued maize and the increasing importation of wheat has meant that the net value of grain trade in China represented a growing outflow of resources up to 1986. In the 1981–1985 period, the average annual value of grain exports was $400 million, versus $2.2 billion in grain imports. Analyzing China's grain trade over the entire 25-year period, it appears that gains made in the 1960s and early 1970s have been offset by changes in the late 1970s to 1980s. Thus, considering the whole period, the net value of China's grain imports has increased at 1.7% annually.

What is significant about the 1976–1980 period is that while the net balance in grain trade deteriorated sharply, the effect domestically was to increase the supply of basic grains for popular consumption. Rice exports decreased, and wheat imports rose substantially. There was 5% more rice available and over 15% more wheat. The current policy of substituting maize for rice exports probably means that quantities of rice that were once exported are now available for domestic consumption.

Thus, China has also done remarkably well in terms of increasing its food security. By 1983, it was estimated that the Chinese finally had enough to eat, and that average food availabilities were approximately 2,700 kilocalories and 85 grams of protein. Plant foods supplied 95% of energy and 85% of protein, leading one analyst to characterize the diet as monotonous (Smil 1985:273). However that may be, China has sufficient food for its population of over a billion people, and it appears that inequalities in access to food are relatively small. About one-seventh of state income currently subsidizes the production and consumption of foodstuffs (Smil 1985:273). Were the government to relax its emphasis on grain production (which ensures that 80% of cropland is devoted to grain crops), it is likely that inequalities among producers and consumers would increase. The country's food situation would then look much like others in this study in which a varied and meat-rich diet for some would be accompanied by undernutrition for others.

At the present time, meat consumption is increasing in China mainly in the form of pork—per capita availability is about 12 kilograms per year. Most of this is produced from more than 300 million pigs raised in backyard production units; balanced livestock feeds are little used in China, with production only 4.5 million tons in 1983 (Smil 1985:250). Use of grain for animal feed is increasing; most estimates are that it rose from about 5.7% of total output in the 1950s to over 10% in the late 1970s (Walker 1984:178). In comparison with other countries in our study, however, thus far China has put most of its emphasis on producing food for people rather than feed for animals. In addition, the government has resisted importing more grain as a solution to the deficit of feed grains (Walker 1984:194).

8

Directions for
Further Research

The results presented in this book are intended as a first step in a larger research project. We have been able to identify the countrywide and global changes that are occurring in the substitution of grains. We have been able to demonstrate the magnitude of these changes, and we believe that further research is warranted on the social and political policies that have accelerated the substitutions in grain production as well as on the socioeconomic impacts of these changes on producers and consumers. This research should take the form of more extensive case studies within the countries that we have covered in this book. In each regional analysis, we have suggested further ideas and topics that require investigation.

In a more general vein, we believe that the research that we have carried out in Mexico and the results presented here suggest some larger hypotheses and premises that require wide attention and further investigation. Accordingly, in this final chapter, we present some speculations to contribute to the ongoing discussions about the evolution of the world grain economy.

THE GREEN REVOLUTION,
GRAIN SUBSTITUTION, AND POOR PEOPLE

The research reported in this book should be considered part of a larger literature on the impact of modernization and international economic integration on the welfare of the people in rural areas of developing countries. Time and again, authors have reported on the ravaging impact of these processes on rural society and individual well-being throughout the Third World (Hewitt de Alcántara 1976; Barkin 1982; Franke and Chasin 1980; Kolko 1988; Lipton 1988). Our early work in Mexico documented what has now become a classic case of impoverishment as a result of the blind adherence to liberal dogma of the beneficence of the marketplace in resolving society's problems. The present study reinforces our initial hypothesis that the Mexican experience is not unique; rather, it is one of the most poignant examples of incorrect policymaking in the name of modernization and international economic integration.

How can such a broad gap persist between the literature that celebrates the green revolution and that which laments the "second generation effects," as these welfare issues are called? The development and introduction of modern varieties (MVs) had a revolutionary potential: By introducing new seeds and production, the massive international agricultural research programs imagined that they could increase the supply of food, raise rural incomes, and end hunger throughout the world. There was much evidence to support their assumption: after all, the new plants were much more efficient processors of water, nutrients, and energy. These new varieties produce higher yields and can provide cheaper food from plants better suited to resist environmental threats. As a leading World Bank analyst summarizes this optimistic point of view: "The bio-economic impact of MVs should be especially favorable to smaller farmers, hired workers, and poor consumers" (Lipton 1988).

But now it is widely recognized that this promise has been barely tapped. The insightful and path-breaking but controversial critiques of an earlier period (Pearse 1980; George 1977; Moore Lappé and Collins 1977) have now become incorporated into a more conventional wisdom; the same World Bank analyst cited above points out that "much of this 'pro-poor potential' has been lost due to (a) insertion of MVs into social systems favoring urban groups and the big farmers who supply them, (b) demographic dynamics making labor cheaper relative to land, and (c) research structures prioritizing fashionable topics rather than genuine needs of the poor" (Lipton 1988). Another analysis of a part of the international agricultural research community illustrates the way in which these various factors have contributed to an agricultural economy ill-suited to respond to the world's pressing nutritional problems (Jennings 1988).

However, the problem of the substitution of grains on a global scale goes beyond the problem of ill-placed priorities. As this book has vividly illustrated, national governments seem determined to exacerbate the problem by developing policies that deliberately discriminate against small farmers and poor people's food. The patterns of production and trade illustrated in the brief country studies oblige us to reject the idea that these events are simply the result of misinformed or misguided governments. We suggest that the systematic changes in cropping patterns documented here are the predictable result of the same interaction of market forces and technology with political structures that so deformed the green revolution, impeding society from enjoying the social fruits inherent in the biological potential of the new technology.

This book also echoes the clarion call of numerous case studies: The transition from traditional agriculture to commercial crops not only threatens the social integrity of entire societies and the long-run economic viability of many nations but, just as ominously, appears to be irreversible. Repeatedly, throughout the world and in greatly differing cultures, we observed that where traditional food crops are being displaced, so too are small-scale food producers. With this process, social structures disintegrate as their rural productive bases erode and people are inexorably driven into unproductive urban quicksands. More research is needed to pinpoint these processes and to contribute to the urgent task of developing alternative approaches to policymaking.

FOOD SELF-SUFFICIENCY
VERSUS COMPARATIVE ADVANTAGE

We also believe that the kind of research we are doing and that we are advocating fits into the lively and growing debate over whether developing countries should pursue economic development through the modernization of agriculture based on the model of comparative advantage. This book aims at contributing to that discussion by providing an analysis of long-term trends in selected developing countries and hopes to stimulate future case studies to assess the socioeconomic impact of growth along the lines of comparative advantage. Our research suggests that the implementation of the comparative advantage model decreases the likelihood that a country will achieve or maintain food self-sufficiency.[32]

In those developing countries where agriculture is increasingly oriented toward the production of specialized commodities for world markets, economic development follows the policy dictates of the model of comparative advantage. That model posits that a developing area will improve its economic position most effectively by taking advantage of its unique resources (a constellation of soils, climate, and vegetation for agricultural production, or mineral wealth, or proximity to markets, etc.) and productive knowledge and by developing specialized production based on the exploitation of those particular resources (for a comprehensive discussion of this theory, see Leamer [1984]).

According to this model, a country or region will enjoy a higher rate of sustained growth by specializing in the production of those goods in which it is relatively most efficient, exporting these commodities, and using the proceeds to import what it does not produce itself. Presumably, if each region is producing the commodities for which it has a comparative advantage, then each commodity will be produced with the most efficient use of resources and will be available in the world marketplace at the least cost.

The model assumes that the dislocations occasioned by a decrease in local production of some commodities and consequent increase in imports of those commodities will be more than offset by the more efficient production of the particular commodity for which the region is uniquely suited. Accordingly, if one accepts the premises of the model of comparative advantage, a decline in food self-sufficiency is not, per se, a threat to a region's economic stability or progress: It may simply import that which it does not produce itself, presumably at a lower direct cost (in terms of the resources needed to produce the commodities put in its stead) than if the commodity were produced locally.

Economic development along the lines of comparative advantage is driven by policies promoting the opening of national economies to world trade and the modernization of agriculture. New production technologies are expected to allow the region to take greater advantage of its resources by improving productivity. The heavy investment necessary to modernize and develop specialized production, however, means that most small-scale producers cannot take part in this development process. Other sectors of the economy may also go relatively undeveloped or be left to stagnate.

Agricultural modernization takes place in a variety of ways, with different crops in distinct regions, with the participation of various social groups. To proceed, it does not necessarily require, although it is frequently accelerated by, the overt modernization policies of national governments and international aid agencies. In Latin America, modernization generally leads to the displacement of maize, the region's most important basic staple; in Africa, barley, sorghum, millet, or maize, and certain noncereal food crops are displaced, depending on the region. In Asia, sorghum, millet, or rice may be lost.

Economic growth through specialization dictated by the application of policies consistent with the theory of comparative advantage introduces a developing country into a contradictory process of standardization and differentiation in the production sector. In the agricultural sphere, we observe a standardization of the commodities themselves as the producers flock to the latest openings in international markets. To remain competitive, the growers adopt standardized production processes, including planting seeds of internationally traded varieties, and the complementary package of agrochemical inputs usually required to meet market norms for insect and disease control and cosmetic standards. As this standardized production expands, competitive pressures motivate some producers and countries to search for new product lines and production technologies to expand market shares and increase profit margins. In food production, this may take the form of improved varieties or new genetic strains, or methods for, or forms of, processed foods. Thus, agricultural trade leads to a continual expansion of specialization in which those producers who follow the leaders will find themselves in markets where intense international competition will continually bring downward pressures to bear on prices, thus making what seemed to be profitable trading opportunities simply average profit centers.

Scientific advances influence this process. Improved varieties of grains such as sorghum and wheat, for example, were developed in such a way that they were adaptable over a very wide range of soil and climatic conditions, provided certain modern inputs were available. These advances allowed the standardized production of these grains to spread over major areas of the world where their production was previously unfeasible (Vocke 1986; House 1985). Almost invariably, however, their introduction requires significant increases in the costs of cultivation, so that the traditional group of farmers is no longer able to afford production. This problem is exacerbated by the lack of success in developing new varieties for small-scale farmers in resource-poor ecological conditions prevailing in the Third World. For example, scientists have not developed widely adaptable varieties of maize, and so those that exist are suited to relatively specific environmental conditions, with little attention being given to the problems occasioned by the limited resources that most maize farmers in the developing countries have at their disposal.

THE ROLE OF NATIONAL
AND INTERNATIONAL FOOD POLICIES

Government and multilateral aid policies aimed at modernizing agriculture and promoting export-oriented crops, such as those based on the theory of comparative advantage, will encourage the transfer of land to commercial agriculture. That is, those producers who have access to the necessary financial resources will take advantage of government-sponsored irrigation projects and credit or subsidies for improved technology, high yielding varieties of seed, fertilizers, and other inputs in order to increase their productivity. National development policies tend to discriminate against traditional grain producers as they seek to increase agricultural output and export earnings. These earnings from the agricultural sector are then expected to finance industrial development.

Thus, producers of traditional staples often cannot participate in government programs, either because the programs explicitly exclude crops that do not have a high market value or because the producers themselves lack access to the necessary resources (or the institutions that can provide them) and thus cannot take advantage of the incentives. In contrast, official policies that specifically promote food production by targeting producers of basic cereals have the effect of slowing the transformation of agriculture (toward export and luxury crops) and maintaining or even increasing the amount of land dedicated to basic food crops.

Consumer-oriented development policies frequently attempt to hold down basic staple prices as part of an industrial development program, in order to allow the urban population to subsist on relatively low wages. In this way, agriculture is used to subsidize industrial development at the consumer end as well. By discriminating against basic grain producers in these ways, however, the artificially low market prices discourage them from expanding production to meet the needs of the growing urban population. In many instances, producers respond by reducing the amount of land in production so that they cover only their own subsistence needs; or they may abandon cultivation altogether and enter the wage-working (and consuming) population; in either case the pressure on the country's balance of payments and on the urban areas that receive the resulting migration is clearly harmful to growth.[33]

Consequently, unless price and other consumer-oriented policies designed to make more food available cheaply are accompanied by policies to support producers, they will have the contradictory effect of decreasing internal supply—because they both decrease the number of producers and swell the ranks of consumers. Governments, in turn, respond by importing more basic foodstuffs—often at much higher prices (and/or social costs) than if these foods were grown domestically—or by using scarce and erroneously priced foreign exchange. They must also search for new ways of earning foreign exchange monies to finance imports. One important primary target of such export promotion campaigns is to further modernize agriculture; that is, to transfer resources from basic food to export production.

The potential negative impacts of the process of substitution in agricultural production through the model of comparative advantage occur at several different levels. First, large-scale dependence on foreign food imports subjects a country to instability caused by variations in policies of other countries or in international supplies and prices. A recent example of this is the dramatic rise in the international prices of some dairy products caused by the changes in policies (reduction in subsidies) within the European Common Market and the United States. In the event of a reduction in global production resulting from policy or from economic or natural causes, the increased prices may cause a serious deterioration in a country's external position, or even place the importing country's neediest groups in danger because of their inability to obtain basic necessities. In extreme cases, for example during international crises or war, it may mean that major portions of the population face food shortages or starvation. This, in fact, occurred in Mexico during World War II, when that country converted almost 25% of its land in maize to the production of oilseed crops needed by the United States for its war effort. As a result, large portions of the Mexican population faced starvation. U.S. officials even objected to exporting maize to Mexico to help offset the crisis (Niblo 1988).[34]

Second, even if economic development through the comparative advantage model is more efficient than other strategies are, it does not take into account the differential impacts of modernization on producers and consumers, and/or subgroups within these categories. In the process of modernization, small producers are squeezed out, their land abandoned or absorbed into larger, more capitalized enterprises. They lose the source of their livelihood and become part of an increasing population of urban and rural wage workers. Developing countries frequently, however, do not have the capacity to absorb these displaced producers and thus cannot effectively use their human resources. Nor do they have the ability to obligate the beneficiaries of specialization to compensate the losers from such a restructuring.[35] The resulting disadvantaged and/or unemployed population, with little income and unstable living conditions, is the group most vulnerable to hunger and malnutrition. Moreover, the increased polarization between rich and poor may engender major social and political upheavals that may constitute a major long-term drain on the country's economic and political resources.

Robinson's (1979:102–103) critique of free trade and comparative advantage is appropriate in this context. She points out that the benefits of these policies depend on two assumptions, neither of which holds in the modern world. First, the argument is made in terms of comparisons of static equilibrium conditions in which each trading nation is characterized by full employment of resources and balanced payments. It is obvious that this condition does not hold. Second, because all countries are treated as having the same level of development, unequal exchange is not part of the model. The deteriorating terms of trade for most exports of developing countries make it quite clear that this assumption is invalid.

It is especially critical that the model of comparative advantage does not take into consideration economies, such as those of most of the developing world, where there is significant underutilization of resources. In such instances, it is not an either/or proposition for resource development. For example, workers whom the economy is unable to absorb when displaced into the modern sector may have been contributing to overall economic growth, even if they were not producing at an "optimum" level of productivity. Commercial production often does not have a need for either the same lands or laborers that are required for basic food production on small farms under rainfed conditions. This is frequently the case in Third World countries where the financial and other resources needed for luxury and export production are simply not available to small-scale food producers.

Consumers are also differentially affected by this transformation in agricultural production: There is relatively less low cost food available to low income populations, both rural and urban. Research has demonstrated, for example, that hunger and malnutrition are frequently not a result of the lack of food production or even supplies, but of poor people's lack of income to buy food. Sen (1981) shows that in major famines in various parts of the world, for example in Ethiopia and Bangladesh in the early 1970s, food availability was not a problem. Rather, people did not have money to buy food. Similarly, García (1981) shows that the social impact of drought—even in the absence of aid—is the direct result of social structures that deny resources to particular groups rather than any necessity for mass famine. Thus, major portions of the population of developing countries cannot realize the benefits from development based on the exploitation of resources and the specialization dictated by the theory of comparative advantage.

Further investigation of such phenomena as grain substitution is required to advance our knowledge and understanding of this complex and crucially important debate. Research and development efforts to address the welfare needs of small and medium-sized agricultural producers are likely to be ineffective if the overall trends in global food and agricultural policy continue to be based on a premise that is detrimental to the interests of these producers.

Our purpose in this book was to undertake a disaggregated consideration of the substitution of grains in world production and trade. The results of our analysis of the trends in the FAO data and of secondary literature on a large number of countries have indicated that there are important reasons for doing comparative analyses that focus on trends in countries and even in regions within countries. We will consider our endeavor a success if we have stimulated further interest among those who are willing to undertake the more intensive case studies we are advocating.

Tables

All tables are based on FAO data, FAO, *Production and Trade Yearbooks*, 1961–1986, as provided on magnetic media, Rome, 1987, except the following:

Table XV is based on information in Cheryl Williamson Gray, *Food Consumption Parameters for Brazil,* Report No. 32 (Washington, D.C.: IFPRI, September 1982), p.17.

Table XVI presents data adapted from Douglas Graham, Howard Gauthier, and José Roberto Mendonca de Barros, "Thirty Years of Agricultural Growth in Brazil: Crop Performance, Regional Profile, and Recent Policy Review," *Economic Development and Cultural Change* 36, No. 1 (October 1987): 8. Our analysis relies on the in-country data compiled by FIBGE because it appears more reliable than the FAO data, particularly with respect to the relationship between cereal and noncereal production, which the FAO data show to be relatively constant. Several studies using different methodologies and based on the FIBGE data show that export crops have expanded dramatically in relation to cereal crops. See, for example, Fernando Homem de Melo, *Brazil and the CGIAR Centers: A Study in Their Collaboration in Agricultural Research* (Washington, DC: World Bank, 1986); Ademar Ribeiro Romeiro, "Alternative Developments in Brazil," in *The Green Revolution Revisited,* ed. Bernhard Glasser (London: Allen & Unwin, 1987); and Cheryl Williamson Gray, *Food Consumption Parameters for Brazil,* Report No. 32 (Washington, DC: IFPRI, 1982). The FAO and FIBGE data are more consistent with respect to the changing composition of grain production, for example, in the relative increase in wheat and decrease in maize production during the period in question.

Table XLV is based on information in Chaiwat Konjing and Apisith Issari Yanukala, "Output Demand and Marketing of Rice and Upland Crops in Thailand," in Panaytou, ed. *Food Policy Analysis in Thailand* (Bangkok: Allied, 1985), p. 110.

Table I
Regional Coverage of the Area and Production
of Grains in the Study
(Percentage)

	World	Developed Market	USSR	Developing Market	Latin America	Africa	Asia[a]
All Cereals							
% Area	86	100	100	82	87	65	82
% Prod.	88	100	100	85	89	72	82
Wheat							
% Area	88	100	100	79	86	85	75
% Prod.	88	100	100	84	88	89	81
Maize							
% Area	89	100	100	89	88	63	92
% Prod.	92	100	100	94	88	63	92
Sorghum							
% Area	90	100	100	89	87	61	93
% Prod.	95	100	100	92	94	82	94
Rice							
% Area	82	100	100	82	86	24	82
% Prod.	84	100	100	83	81	43	80
Barley							
% Area	87	100	100	68	72	85	59
% Prod.	87	100	100	73	76	70	64
Oats							
% Area	93	100	100	62	78	94	86
% Prod.	90	100	100	55	79	95	85
Millet							
% Area	79	100	100	77	100	48	94
% Prod.	81	100	100	79	100	53	93
Rye[b]							
% Area		100	100	106	107	101	52
% Prod.		100	100	102	104	104	44

Notes: [a]Excludes the USSR.
[b]Percentages greater than 100 are due to discrepancies in the raw data

Table II
World Distribution of Grain Area and Production by Region, 1961-1986

Grains	Developed Market	USSR	Developing Market	Latin America	Africa	Asia
All Cereals						
Area	22	17	57	7	9	42
Prod.	35	12	48	6	5	40
Wheat						
Area	29	28	40	4	4	33
Prod.	38	23	33	4	2	28
Maize						
Area	32	3	60	21	15	28
Prod.	55	3	36	12	7	19
Sorghum						
Area	14	0	86	8	28	51
Prod.	35	0	65	15	17	66
Rice						
Area	3	0	97	5	3	91
Prod.	7	0	93	4	2	92
Barley						
Area	33	37	25	2	6	17
Prod.	48	29	15	1	3	12
Oats						
Area	50	36	7	2	2	4
Prod.	58	28	5	2	1	3
Millet						
Area	0	7	93	1	33	59
Prod.	0	8	91	1	32	58
Rye						
Area	14	51	4	2	0	6
Prod.	19	42	3	1	0	5

Note: Average shares of grain area (in hectares) and production (in metric tons) as a percentage of the world total.

Table III
Global Distribution of Basic Food Grain Production by Country

Country	Staple Cereal
Latin America	
Argentina	Wheat
Brazil	Rice, Maize
Colombia	Maize
Mexico	Maize
Peru	Maize, Barley
Venezuela	Maize
Southern Asia	
Bangladesh	Rice
India	Rice, Sorghum, Millet
Southeastern Asia	
Indonesia	Rice, Maize
Philippines	Rice, Maize
Thailand	Rice
Eastern Asia	
China	Rice, Maize, Wheat
Central Asia	
USSR	Wheat, Barley
Middle East and Northern Africa	
Algeria	Wheat, Barley
Egypt	Wheat, Sorghum
Morocco	Barley, Wheat
Turkey	Wheat, Barley
Western Africa	
Burkina Faso	Sorghum, Millet
Nigeria	Sorghum, Millet, Maize
Eastern and Southern Africa	
Ethiopia	Wheat
Kenya	Maize, Sorghum, Millet
South Africa	Maize, Sorghum
Sudan	Sorghum, Millet
Tanzania	Maize, Sorghum, Millet
Zimbabwe	Maize, Sorghum, Millet

Table IV
Substitution of Grains in Production by Country, 1961-1986

Country	Increasing Grain	Decreasing Grain	Impact on Staple Grain Production[a]
Latin America			
Argentina	Sorghum	Maize, Barley Oats, Rye	N/A[b]
Brazil	Wheat	Maize, Rice	- 5
Colombia	Sorghum, Rice	Maize, Wheat	-26
Mexico	Sorghum	Maize	-14
Peru	Rice	Barley, Wheat	-16
Venezuela	Sorghum, Rice	Maize	-40
Middle East and Northern Africa			
Algeria	Barley	Wheat	N/A
Egypt	Maize, Rice	Wheat, Sorghum	- 6
Morocco	Barley	Sorghum, Maize, Wheat	N/A
Turkey	Wheat	Rye, Maize, Oats	+ 7
Western Africa			
Burkina Faso	Millet	Maize, Rice	+ 4
Nigeria	Rice	Sorghum, Maize	- 8
Eastern and Southern Africa			
Ethiopia	Maize	Wheat	N/A
Kenya	Maize	Sorghum, Millet	N/A
South Africa	Wheat	Maize, Sorghum	-10
Sudan	Wheat	Sorghum, Millet	- 7[c]
Tanzania	Rice, Sorghum	Maize, Millet	-16
Zimbabwe	Maize, Sorghum	Millet	+18
Southern Asia			
Bangladesh	Wheat	Rice	N/A
India	Wheat	Sorghum, Millet	- 8
Southeastern Asia			
Indonesia	Rice	Maize	+ 7
Philippines	Maize	Rice	-11
Thailand	Maize, Sorghum	Rice	-10
Eastern Asia			
China	Rice, Maize, Wheat	Sorghum, Barley Millet	N/A
Central Asia			
USSR	Barley, Oats	Wheat, Rye	N/A

Notes: [a]This column refers to the percentage of total land cultivated in grains that is affected by the substitution of grains in production. Positive and negative signs refer to the percentages of total grain land shifted to (+) or away from (-) staple food grain production.
 [b]N/A: Signifies countries in which the impact of the shift in composition of grain production on food production appears negligible or is not evident from the FAO data.
 [c]The figures for the Sudan cover 1961-1980.

Table V
Changes in Composition of Grain Production
and Trade by Country, 1961–1986

Country	Increasing Grain	Decreasing Grain	Increasing Grain Imports	Change in Trade[a]
Latin America				
Argentina	Sorghum	Maize, Barley Oats, Rye	Maize	+
Brazil	Wheat	Maize, Rice	Maize	–
Colombia	Sorghum, Rice	Maize, Wheat	Sorghum, Barley	–
Mexico	Sorghum	Maize	Maize, Sorghum	–
Peru	Rice	Barley, Wheat	Maize	–
Venezuela	Sorghum, Rice	Maize	Maize, Sorghum	–
Middle East and Northern Africa				
Algeria	Barley	Wheat	Maize, Barley	–
Egypt	Maize, Rice	Wheat, Sorghum	Maize	–
Morocco	Barley	Sorghum, Maize	Maize	–
Turkey	Wheat	Rye, Maize, Oats	Barley, Rice	+
Western Africa				
Burkina Faso	Millet	Maize	Maize, Sorghum	–
Nigeria	Rice	Sorghum, Maize	Maize, Rice	–
Eastern and Southern Africa				
Ethiopia	Maize	Wheat	Wheat	–
Kenya	Maize	Sorghum, Millet	Wheat	–
South Africa	Wheat	Maize, Sorghum	Maize	+
Sudan	Wheat	Sorghum, Millet	(No Change)	–
Tanzania	Rice, Sorghum	Maize, Millet	Maize, Rice	–
Zimbabwe	Maize, Sorghum	Millet	Maize, Rice	+
Southern Asia				
Bangladesh	Wheat	Rice	Wheat	–
India	Wheat	Sorghum, Millet	Rice	+
Southeastern Asia				
Indonesia	Rice	Maize	Wheat	–
Philippines	Maize	Rice	Maize	–
Thailand	Maize, Sorghum	Rice	Maize, Sorghum	+
Eastern Asia				
China	Rice, Maize Wheat	Sorghum, Barley Millet	Wheat	–
Central Asia				
USSR	Barley, Oats	Wheat	Maize, Sorghum, Barley	–

Note:[a]This column shows whether the country has experienced a net gain (+) or deterioration (–) in its total grain trade balance for the period 1961–1986.

Table VI
Substitution of Grains in Production in Latin America, 1961-1985
(Five-Year Averages)

Country		Increasing Grains (% area cultivated)			Decreasing Grains (% area cultivated)	
		1961-1965	1981-1985		1961-1965	1981-1985
Argentina	Sorghum	8	18	Maize	27	25
				Barley	5	1
				Rye	5	1
Brazil	Wheat	6	11	Maize	62	59
				Rice	30	28
Colombia	Sorghum	1	19	Maize	61	45
	Rice	24	31	Wheat	10	3
Mexico	Sorghum	2	16	Maize	83	69
Peru	Rice	10	26	Wheat	20	11
				Barley	23	14
Venezuela	Sorghum	0	30	Maize	84	45
	Rice	15	25			

Table VII
Growth of Sorghum and Maize Production in Selected Latin American
Countries, Compared with Other Regions

| Country/ Region | % Cultivated Area[a] | | Growth Rates[b] | | |
	1961-1965	1981-1985	Production	Yield	Area
Argentina					
Sorghum	8.1	18.2	6.3	2.5	3.7
Maize	27.0	24.7	3.8	3.0	0.7
Brazil					
Sorghum	0.0	0.7	32.4	-1.3[c]	34.1
Maize	62.4	59.2	3.5	1.3	2.2
Colombia					
Sorghum	1.1	18.6	20.3	0.7	19.6
Maize	60.6	45.4	0.2	1.1	- 0.8
Mexico					
Sorghum	2.4	15.6	13.3	1.6	11.3
Maize	82.6	69.4	3.1	2.7	0.4
Peru					
Sorghum	0.2	1.3	13.0	2.4	10.3
Maize	43.2	45.2	2.3	1.6	0.7
Venezuela					
Sorghum	0.1	29.7	23.7	-0.7	24.4
Maize	84.3	44.8	2.7	2.9	0.0
Latin America					
Sorghum			8.4	2.8	5.5
Maize			3.3	2.2	1.1
Africa					
Sorghum			1.4	0.0	1.4
Maize			2.0	1.2	0.8
Asia					
Sorghum			0.4	1.7	- 1.4
Maize			4.9	3.6	1.3
World					
Sorghum			2.4	2.1	0.3
Maize			3.6	2.7	0.9

Notes: [a]Data refers to percentage of the crop in relation to the total amount
of land in cereal. For example, sorghum occupied 8.1% of all the land sown
in cereals in Argentina during the period 1961-1965.
[b]Annual growth rates for 1961-1986.
[c]Data not significant.

Table VIII
Average Yields and Growth Rates of Major Grains
in Latin American Countries,
1961-1986

Grains	All Latin America	Argen- tina	Brazil	Colom- bia	Mexico	Peru	Vene- zuela
All Cereals							
Avg. Yield	1.6	1.9	1.4	2.0	1.7	1.8	1.6
% Growth	2.1	2.3	1.1	2.9	3.3	2.2	2.8
Wheat							
Avg. Yield	1.5	1.5	0.9	1.2	3.2	1.0	0.4
% Growth	1.8	1.1	3.3	2.5	3.5	0.6	-1.0
Maize							
Avg. Yield	1.6	2.6	1.5	1.3	1.4	1.7	1.1
% Growth	2.2	3.0	1.3	1.1	2.7	1.6	2.9
Sorghum							
Avg. Yield	2.3	2.3	1.5	2.3	2.9	2.8	1.6
% Growth	2.8	2.5	0.5	0.7	1.7	2.4	-0.1
Rice							
Avg. Yield	1.9	3.6	-	3.5	2.8	4.2	2.4
% Growth	1.2	0.4	-	3.7	1.6	0.5	2.1
Barley							
Avg. Yield	-	-	-	-	-	0.9	-
% Growth	-	-	-	-	-	0.4	-

Notes: [a]Data refers to percentage of the crop in relation to the total amount
of land in cereal. For example, sorghum occupied 8.1% of all the land sown
in cereals in Argentina during the period 1961-1965.
[b]Annual growth rates for 1961-1986.
[c]Data not significant.

Table IX
Composition of Grain Imports to Selected Countries
in Latin America, 1961-1985
(As a Percentage of Total Grain Imports)

Country		Increasing Grains			Decreasing Grains	
		1961-1965	1981-1985		1961-1965	1981-1985
Argentina	Maize	1	37	Sorghum	99	27
Brazil	Maize	0	6	Wheat	98	87
Colombia	Sorghum	0	9	Wheat	88	70
	Barley	0	13			
Mexico	Sorghum	23	48	Barley	25	1
	Maize	35	38			
Peru	Maize	3	25	Wheat	88	67
Venezuela	Maize	9	42	Wheat	88	35
	Sorghum	0	23			

Table X
Value of Net Grain Trade for Selected Countries
in Latin America, 1961-1985
(Five-Year Averages in Thousands of Current U.S. Dollas)

Country	1961-1965	1966-1970	1971-1975	1976-1980	1981-1985
Argentina	375,552	440,929	835,616	1,430,873	2,406,020
Brazil	-153,099	-122,648	-229,579	- 749,692	- 939,508
Colombia	- 17,217	- 19,400	- 52,471	- 91,187	- 147,875
Mexico	17,707	40,865	-266,519	- 474,102	- 689,955
Peru	- 39,353	- 50,433	- 89,921	- 189,678	- 226,177
Venezuela	- 34,018	- 45,587	-130,917	- 318,742	- 433,867

Table XI
Colombia: Grain Area, Yields, and Production
(25-Year Averages and Growth Rates, 1961-1986)

Crop	Area		Yield		Production	
	Average %	% Increase	Average MT	% Increase	Average MT	% Increase
Cereal						
Grains	100	0.3	2.0	2.9	2,508	3.2
Sorghum	10	19.6	2.3	0.7	296	20.9
Rice	27	1.4	3.5	3.7	1,216	5.2
Maize	54	- 0.8	1.3	1.1	832	0.2
Wheat	5	- 4.9	1.2	2.5	75	- 2.6

Note: Average area is the share of a grain in terms of total cultivated are
of cereals; average yield is in metric tons/ha; average MT is in thousands
All growth rates are annualized averages for whole 1961-1986 period.

Table XII
Mexico: Grain Area, Yields, and Production
(25-Year Averages and Growth Rates, 1961-1986)

Crop	Area		Yield		Production	
	Average %	% Increase	Average MT	% Increase	Average MT	% Increase
Cereal						
Grains	100	1.2	1.7	3.3	16,466	4.6
Sorghum	11	11.3	2.9	1.7	3,189	13.3
Maize	75	0.4	1.4	2.7	9,684	3.1
Wheat	9	1.6	3.2	3.5	2,706	5.2

Note: Average area is the share of a grain in terms of total cultivated are
of cereals; average yield is in metric tons/ha; average MT is in thousands
All growth rates are annualized averages for whole 1961-1986 period.

Table XIII
Venezuela: Grain Area, Yields, and Production
(25-Year Averages and Growth Rates, 1961-1986)

Crop	Area		Yield		Production	
	Average %	% Increase	Average MT	% Increase	Average MT	% Increase
Cereal						
Grains	100	2.4	1.6	2.8	1,096	1.2
Sorghum	12	26.7	1.6	-0.7	172	26.0
Rice	19	3.6	2.4	2.3	326	6.0
Maize	69	0.0	1.3	2.9	596	2.7

Note: Average area is the share of a grain in terms of total cultivated area
of cereals; average yield is in metric tons/ha; average MT is in thousands.
All growth rates are annualized averages for whole 1961-1986 period.

Table XIV
Argentina: Grain Area, Yields, and Production
(25-Year Averages and Growth Rates, 1961-1986)

Crop	Area		Yield		Production	
	Average %	% Increase	Average MT	% Increase	Average MT	% Increase
Cereal						
Grains	95	0.5	1.9	2.3	22,451	2.8
Sorghum	15	3.7	2.3	2.5	4,333	6.3
Wheat	45	0.7	1.5	1.1	8,131	1.9
Maize	27	0.7	2.6	3.0	8,115	3.8
Barley	3	-7.3	1.3	1.7	471	-6.2
Rye	3	-6.3	0.8	1.0	392	-6.3

Note: Average area is the share of a grain in terms of total cultivated area
of cereals; average yield is in metric tons/ha; average MT is in thousands.
All growth rates are annualized averages for whole 1961-1986 period.

Table XV
Consumption of Basic Foods in Brazil by Income Level
(Percentages)

Food	Lowest 15%		Lowest 30%		Highest 70%	
	Rural	Urban	Rural	Urban	Rural	Urban
Cassava	34.5	15.6	31.5	11.2	10.4	2.1
Beans	24.0	12.5	21.7	11.5	13.9	7.7
Rice	8.8	17.2	11.2	20.0	19.1	19.4
Maize	6.0	3.2	7.2	2.7	7.6	1.6
Wheat	1.6	10.2	1.8	10.0	10.4	10.2
% of Total Calories	74.9	58.7	73.4	55.4	61.4	41.0

Table XVI
Brazil: Average Annual Growth Rates for Selected Crops,
1960-1980
(Percentages)

Crop	Area		Yield		Production	
	1960-1970	1970-1980	1960-1970	1970-1980	1960-1970	1970-1980
Staples						
Wheat	6.9	5.6	2.0	1.1	11.8	6.9
Rice	4.3	3.1	- 1.5	- 0.3	2.8	2.7
Cassava	4.3	0.2	1.2	- 2.4	5.5	- 2.2
Maize	3.9	1.3	0.9	1.3	4.8	2.6
Beans	3.8	1.9	- 0.3	- 4.6	3.5	- 2.7
Others						
Soybeans	17.1	17.5	0.8	1.1	17.9	18.6
Oranges	5.5	8.8	0.7	3.0	6.1	11.8
Sugarcane	2.3	4.5	0.9	2.4	3.2	7.0
Tobacco	1.2	4.1	3.0	2.7	4.2	6.8
Cotton	2.6	- 2.2	- 1.9	- 2.6	0.7	- 4.8
Cacao	- 1.0	0.4	4.6	5.2	3.6	5.6
Coffee	- 7.7	- 0.1	- 1.4	- 3.0	0.8	- 4.8

Consumption
of Basic
Foods

Table XVII
Area, Yields, and Production
es and Growth Rates, 1961-1986)

			Yield		Production	
C:		erage MT		% Increase	Average MT	% Increase
Ce.						
Gi		0.1	1.8	2.2	1,453	2.3
Ric	16	4.2	4.2	0.5	543	4.7
Whe..c	16	-2.5	1.0	0.6	120	-1.9
Maize	45	0.7	1.7	1.6	603	2.3
Barley	20	-2.9	0.9	0.4	149	-2.4

Note: Average area is the share of a grain in terms of total cultivated area
of cereals; average yield is in metric tons/ha; average MT is in thousands.
All growth rates are annualized averages for whole 1961-1986 period.

Table XVIII
Substitution of Grains in Production
in Northern Africa and the Middle East, 1961-1985
(Five-Year Averages)

Country		Increasing Grains (% Area Cultivated)		Decreasing Grains (% Area Cultivated)	
		1961-1965	1981-1985	1961-1965	1981-1985
Algeria	Barley	29	34	Wheat	69	61
	Oats	2	5			
Egypt	Maize	37	42	Wheat	30	27
				Millet	11	8
				Rice	24[a]	20
Morocco	Barley	42	48	Wheat	41	40
				Maize	12	9
				Sorghum	3	1
Turkey	Wheat	61	68	Rye	5	2
				Oats	3	1

Note: [a]Average acreage, 1966-1970.

Table XIX
Composition of Grain Imports to Selected Countries
in Northern Africa and the Middle East, 1961-1985
(As a Percentage of Total Grain Imports)

Country		Increasing Grains			Decreasing Grains	
		1961-1965	1981-1985		1961-1965	1981-1985
Algeria	Maize	1	11	Wheat	91	79
Egypt	Maize	11	19	Wheat	89	81
Morocco	Maize	1	7	Barley	10	4
Turkey	Barley	0	27	Wheat	98	63
	Rice	0	6			

Table XX
Value of Net Grain Trade for Selected Countries
in Northern Africa and the Middle East, 1961-1985
(Five-Year Averages in Thousands of Current U.S. Dollars)

Country	1961-1965	1966-1970	1971-1975	1976-1980	1981-1985
Algeria	-23,842	-46,789	-190,765	-519,385	- 784,390
Egypt	-92,998	-46,250	-339,571	-766,971	-1,606,882
Morocco	-14,454	-35,469	-137,514	-238,058	- 364,918
Turkey	-38,768	-24,840	- 88,529	104,539	34,579

Table XXI
Turkey: Grain Area, Yields, and Production
(25-Year Averages and Growth Rates, 1961-1986)

	Area		Yield		Production	
Crop	Average %	% Increase	Average MT	% Increase	Average MT	% Increase
Cereal						
Grains	94	0.3	1.5	2.3	20,517	2.7
Wheat	66	0.8	1.5	2.4	13,208	3.2
Barley	21	0.8	1.6	2.4	4,488	2.7

Note: Average area is the share of a grain in terms of total cultivated area
of cereals; average yield is in metric tons/ha; average MT is in thousands.
All growth rates are annualized averages for whole 1961-1986 period.

Table XXII
Algeria: Grain Area, Yields, and Production
(25-Year Averages and Growth Rates, 1961-1986)

	Area		Yield		Production	
Crop	Average %	% Increase	Average MT	% Increase	Average MT	% Increase
Cereal						
Grains	100	0.0	0.6	1.2	1,867	1.2
Wheat	69	-0.5	0.6	1.0	1,260	0.4
Barley	28	0.5	0.6	1.9	544	2.5

Note: Average area is the share of a grain in terms of total cultivated area
of cereals; average yield is in metric tons/ha; average MT is in thousands.
All growth rates are annualized averages for whole 1961-1986 period.

Table XXIII
Morocco: Grain Area, Yields, and Production
(25-Year Averages and Growth Rates, 1961-1986)

Crop	Area		Yield		Production	
	Average %	% Increase	Average MT	% Increase	Average MT	% Increase
Cereal Grains	98	1.1	0.9	1.6	4,149	2.8
Barley	45	1.7	0.9	1.1	1,886	3.1
Wheat	41	1.0	1.0	2.4	1,795	3.5
Maize	10	-0.6	0.7	0.0	323	0.0

Note: Average area is the share of a grain in terms of total cultivated area of cereals; average yield is in metric tons/ha; average MT is in thousands. All growth rates are annualized averages for whole 1961-1986 period.

Table XXIV
Egypt: Grain Area, Yields, and Production
(25-Year Averages and Growth Rates, 1961-1986)

Crop	Area		Yield		Production	
	Average %	% Increase	Average MT	% Increase	Average MT	% Increase
Cereal Grains	88	0.1	3.9	1.5	7,510	1.6
Maize	38	0.6	3.7	2.4	2,694	3.1
Wheat	28	-0.7	3.1	1.6	1,701	0.9
Rice	12	0.6	5.4	0.6	2,263	1.1
Millet[a]	10	-1.0	3.8	0.2	732	-0.8

Notes: Average area is the share of a grain in terms of total cultivated area of cereals; average yield is in metric tons/ha; average MT is in thousands. All growth rates are annualized averages for whole 1961-1986 period.

[a]Includes sorghum.

Table XXV
Burkina Faso: Grain Area, Production, and Trade, 1961-1986
(Five Year Averages)

	1961-1965	1966-1970	1971-1975	1976-1980	1981-1985
Area[a]	1,898	2,048	2,047	1,999	2,117
Production[b]	901	1,044	987	1,101	1,245
Imports[b]	9	21	41	43	60
Exports[b]	0	1	1	1	3

Notes: [a]Area is expressed in thousands of hectares.
[b]Production, imports, and exports are expressed in thousands of metric tons.

Table XXVI
Burkina Faso: Grain Area, Yields, and Production
(25-Year Averages and Growth Rates, 1961-1985)

Crop	Area		Yield		Production	
	Average %	% Increase	Average MT	% Increase	Average MT	% Increase
Cereal Grains	97	0.7	0.5	1.8	2,039	2.6
Maize	7	-0.5	0.7	2.0	130	1.6
Sorghum	51	0.6	0.6	1.8	1,047	2.4
Millet	39	1.3	0.4	1.9	363	3.3

Note: Average area is the share of a grain in terms of total cultivated area of cereals; average yield is in metric tons/ha; average MT is in thousands. All growth rates are annualized averages for whole 1961-1986 period.

Table XXVII
Nigeria: Grain Area, Yields, and Production
(25-Year Averages and Growth Rates, 1961-1986)

Crop	Area Average %	Area % Increase	Yield Average MT	Yield % Increase	Production Average MT	Production % Increase
Cereal						
Grains	100	-0.3	0.9	1.7	8,385	1.4
Sorghum	46	-0.3	0.9	1.0	3,769	0.7
Millet	41	-0.3	0.7	1.6	2,934	1.3
Maize	9	-2.7	1.2	3.7	992	0.9
Rice	4	6.1	1.6	2.7	618	8.9

Note: Average area is the share of a grain in terms of total cultivated are
of cereals; average yield is in metric tons/ha; average MT is in thousands
All growth rates are annualized averages for whole 1961-1986 period.

Table XXVIII
Substitution of Grains in Production
in Sub-Saharan Africa, 1961-1985
(Five-Year Averages)

Country		Increasing Grains (% Area Cultivated) 1961-1965	Increasing Grains (% Area Cultivated) 1981-1985		Decreasing Grains (% Area Cultivated) 1961-1965	Decreasing Grains (% Area Cultivated) 1981-1985
Western Africa						
Burkina						
Faso[a]	Millet	38	42	Maize	8	6
Nigeria	Rice	1	7	Maize	12	6
Eastern Africa						
Ethiopia	Maize	14	16	Wheat	16	14
Sudan	Wheat	1[b]	6	Sorghum	71	64[b]
Kenya	Maize	75	79	Sorghum	11	8
				Millet	5	3
Tanzania	Sorghum	13	24	Maize	66	51
	Rice	7	11			
Southern Africa						
Zimbabwe	Maize	60	73	Millet	32	14
South						
Africa	Wheat	20	27	Maize	70	61

Note: [a]In Burkina Faso, sorghum cultivation has been stable at between 50
and 53% of total grain area throughout the 25 year period.
[b]Figures are for 1976-1980.

Table XXIX
Substitution of Grains in Production and Trade
in Sub-Saharan Africa, 1961-1985
(Percentage of Volume)

Country		Increasing Production (% Area Cultivated)			Increasing Exports[a] (% of Total Exports)	
		1961-1965	1981-1985		1961-1965	1981-1985
Kenya	Maize	75	79	Maize	27	64
Tanzania	Sorghum	13	24	Sorghum	0	15[b]
	Rice	7	11	Rice	36	48[b]
Zimbabwe	Maize	60	73	Maize	77	98
South Africa	Wheat	20	27	Wheat	0	18

Note: [a]Sub-Saharan countries not included in table: Burkina Faso has no grain exports; those of Nigeria are negligible. Ethiopia's exports of wheat, sorghum, and maize were small until the mid 1970s, when they dropped to virtually zero. Sudan's grain exports, which have increased erratically between 1961-1986, consist almost entirely of sorghum, supplemented by millet.
[b]Figures are for 1976-1980. Tanzania's exports dropped to zero after 1980.

Table XXX
Composition of Grain Imports to Selected Countries
in Sub-Saharan Africa, 1961-1985
(As a Percentage of Total Grain Imports)

Country		Increasing Grains			Decreasing Grains	
		1961-1965	1981-1985		1961-1965	1981-1985
Eastern Africa[a]						
Ethiopia	Wheat	82	92	Rice	17	3
Kenya	Wheat	31	47	Maize	54	43
Tanzania	Maize	31	49	Wheat	53	26
	Rice	16	24			
Zimbabwe	Maize	8	15	Wheat	87	67
	Rice	3	15			
Western Africa						
Burkina Faso	Sorghum	0	25	Wheat	90	52
	Maize	10	23			
Nigeria	Rice	1	25	Wheat	98	66
	Maize	0	8			
South Africa	Maize	0	45	Wheat	53	28

Sudan not included because the composition of grain imports has been constant between 1961-1986; wheat constitutes over 95% of grain imports, with rice comprising the remainder.

Table XXXI
Value of Net Grain Trade for Selected Countries
in Sub-Saharan Africa, 1961-1985
(Five-Year Averages in Thousands of Current U.S. Dollars)

Country	1961-1965	1966-1970	1971-1975	1976-1980	1981-1985
Eastern Africa					
Ethiopia	- 784	- 3,081	- 5,826	-34,117	-72,258
Tanzania	-6,489	- 4,861	-46,433	-35,566	-73,667
Sudan	-3,002	-10,700	-13,803	- 4,356	-57,512
Kenya	3,712	9,591	4,286	- 3,402	-23,882
Southern Africa					
Zimbabwe	1,010	4,060	29,836	24,767	15,828
South Africa	61,930	42,980	223,029	310,333	71,742
Western Africa					
Burkina Faso	- 856	- 1,677	- 6,240	- 9,819	- 12,250
Nigeria	-12,628	-20,996	-67,428	-458,268	-614,258

Table XXXII
Ethiopia: Grain Area, Yields, and Production
(25-Year Averages and Growth Rates, 1961-1986)

	Area		Yield		Production	
Crop	Average %	% Increase	Average MT	% Increase	Average MT	% Increase
Cereal Grains	66	-0.8	0.9	1.7	4,699	0.9
Maize	16	0.2	1.3	2.5	1,028	2.7
Sorghum	19	0.2	1.0	1.1	923	0.5
Wheat	14	-1.1	0.9	2.2	635	0.3
Barley	18	-0.7	0.9	1.7	821	0.9
Millet	5	-1.0	0.7	2.5	169	1.5

Note: Average area is the share of a grain in terms of total cultivated area
of cereals; average yield is in metric tons/ha; average MT is in thousands.
All growth rates are annualized averages for whole 1961-1986 period.

Table XXXIII
Sudan: Grain Area, Yields, and Production
(25-Year Averages and Growth Rates, 1961-1986)

Crop	Area		Yield		Production	
	Average %	% Increase	Average MT	% Increase	Average MT	% Increase
Cereal						
Grains	73	5.2	0.7	-2.3	2,339	2.9
Wheat	4	8.2	1.2	-0.5	148	7.4
Sorghum	68	5.1	0.8	-2.1	1,786	3.1
Millet	27	5.2	0.4	-4.1	373	1.0

Note: Average area is the share of a grain in terms of total cultivated area of cereals; average yield is in metric tons/ha; average MT is in thousands. All growth rates are annualized averages for whole 1961-1986 period.

Table XXXIV
South Africa: Grain Area, Yields, and Production
(25-Year Averages and Growth Rates, 1961-1986)

Crop	Area		Yield		Production	
	Average %	% Increase	Average MT	% Increase	Average MT	% Increase
Cereal						
Grains	99	0.7	1.3	0.6	9,611	1.3
Maize	68	-0.1	1.5	0.7	7,466	0.6
Wheat	22	2.3	1.0	1.7	1,544	4.0

Note: Average area is the share of a grain in terms of total cultivated area of cereals; average yield is in metric tons/ha; average MT is in thousands. All growth rates are annualized averages for whole 1961-1986 period.

Table XXXV
Kenya: Grain Area, Yields, and Production
(25-Year Averages and Growth Rates, 1961-1986)

Crop	Area		Yield		Production	
	Average %	% Increase	Average MT	% Increase	Average MT	% Increase
Cereal						
Grains	98	0.7	1.5	0.7	2,526	1.5
Maize	76	0.9	1.5	0.8	1,990	1.8
Sorghum	11	-0.1	1.0	-1.7	181	-1.8
Millet	4	-1.9	1.5	-3.1	108	-4.5
Wheat	7	1.2	1.6	2.3	185	3.7

Note: Average area is the share of a grain in terms of total cultivated are
of cereals; average yield is in metric tons/ha; average MT is in thousands
All growth rates are annualized averages for whole 1961-1986 period.

Table XXXVI
Tanzania: Grain Area, Yields, and Production
(25-Year Averages and Growth Rates, 1961-1986)

Crop	Area		Yield		Production	
	Average %	% Increase	Average MT	% Increase	Average MT	% Increase
Cereal						
Grains	92	4.0	0.9	1.1	2,052	5.1
Sorghum	20	6.1	0.7	-0.4	339	5.7
Rice	9	5.7	1.3	0.5	268	6.1
Maize	57	3.3	1.0	1.7	1,187	5.0
Millet	12	2.9	0.7	0.2	195	3.0

Note: Average area is the share of a grain in terms of total cultivated are
of cereals; average yield is in metric tons/ha; average MT is in thousands
All growth rates are annualized averages for whole 1961-1986 period.

Table XXXVII
Zimbabwe: Grain Area, Yields, and Production
(25-Year Averages and Growth Rates, 1961-1986)

Crop	Area		Yield		Production	
	Average %	% Increase	Average MT	% Increase	Average MT	% Increase
Cereal Grains	99	1.5	1.2	2.2	1,897	3.8
Wheat	1	17.8	3.8	5.5	98	24.1
Maize	63	2.4	1.5	1.8	1,511	4.2
Sorghum	11	3.0	0.5	-0.8	91	2.4
Millet	24	- 2.3	0.5	0.7	182	- 1.6

Note: Average area is the share of a grain in terms of total cultivated area
of cereals; average yield is in metric tons/ha; average MT is in thousands.
All growth rates are annualized averages for whole 1961-1986 period.

Table XXXVIII
Substitution of Grains in Production in Asia, 1961-1985
(Five-Year Averages)

Country		Increasing Grains (% Area Cultivated)			Decreasing Grains (% Area Cultivated)	
		1961-1965	1981-1985		1961-1965	1981-1985
Southern Asia						
Bangladesh	Wheat	1	5	Rice	99	95
India	Wheat	14	22	Sorghum	19	15
				Millet	20	16
Southeastern Asia						
Indonesia	Rice	71	78	Maize	29	22
Philippines	Maize	39	50	Rice	61	50
Thailand	Maize	6	14	Rice	94	84
Eastern Asia						
China	Rice	31	36	Sorghum	7	3
	Maize	16	20	Millet	8	4
	Wheat	27	32	Barley	4	1

Table XXXIX
Composition of Grain Imports to Selected Countries in Asia, 1961-1985
(As a Percentage of Total Grain Imports)

Country		Increasing Grains			Decreasing Grains	
		1961-1965	1981-1985		1961-1965	1981-1985
Bangladesh	Wheat	44	85	Rice	33	15
				Barley	23	0
India	Rice	10	27	Wheat	87	72
Indonesia	Wheat	10	76	Rice	89	21
Philippines	Maize	0	25	Rice	33	10
China	Wheat	83	91	Barley	7	1

Table XL
Value of Net Grain Trade for Selected Countries
in Asia, 1961-1985
(Five-Year Averages in Thousands of Current U.S. Dollars)

Country	1961-1965	1966-1970	1971-1975	1976-1980	1981-1985
Southern Asia					
Bangladesh	- 67,422	- 108,666	- 284,359	- 218,606	- 280,446
India	- 411,337	- 543,417	- 554,337	- 241,713	- 215,384
Southeastern Asia					
Indonesia	- 106,339	- 114,188	- 323,288	- 696,531	- 405,838
Philippines	- 60,149	- 48,597	- 112,148	- 101,075	- 207,610
Thailand	216,223	247,581	438,548	899,909	1,340,665
Eastern Asia					
China	- 345,806	- 131,871	- 151,038	-1,198,198	-1,886,058

Table XLI
Bangladesh: Grain Area, Yields, and Production
(25-Year Averages and Growth Rates, 1961-1986)

Crop	Area Average %	Area % Increase	Yield Average MT	Yield % Increase	Production Average MT	Production % Increase
Cereal Grains	99	0.9	1.8	1.3	18,577	2.2
Rice	97	0.7	1.8	1.3	18,123	2.0
Wheat	2	10.1	1.2	5.5	388	16.2

Note: Average area is the share of a grain in terms of total cultivated area
of cereals; average yield is in metric tons/ha; average MT is in thousands.
All growth rates are annualized averages for whole 1961-1986 period.

Table XLII
India: Grain Area, Yields, and Production
(25-Year Averages and Growth Rates, 1961-1986)

Crop	Area Average %	Area % Increase	Yield Average MT	Yield % Increase	Production Average MT	Production % Increase
Cereal Grains	99	0.5	1.2	2.3	120,369	2.8
Rice	38	0.6	1.7	1.7	67,420	2.4
Wheat	18	2.5	1.3	3.6	25,531	6.2
Maize	6	1.1	1.1	1.3	6,111	2.4
Millet	20	-0.5	0.5	0.9	8,984	0.4
Sorghum	17	-0.6	0.6	1.4	9,912	0.7

Note: Average area is the share of a grain in terms of total cultivated area
of cereals; average yield is in metric tons/ha; average MT is in thousands.
All growth rates are annualized averages for whole 1961-1986 period.

Table XLIII
Philippines: Grain Area, Yields, and Production
(25-Year Averages and Growth Rates, 1961-1985)

Crop	Area		Yield		Production	
	Average %	% Increase	Average MT	% Increase	Average MT	% Increase
Cereal Grains	100	1.3	1.4	2.6	8,558	4.0
Rice	55	0.3	1.8	3.3	6,131	3.6
Maize	45	2.6	0.9	2.3	2,419	4.9

Note: Average area is the share of a grain in terms of total cultivated area
of cereals; average yield is in metric tons/ha; average MT is in thousands.
All growth rates are annualized averages for whole 1961-1985 period.

Table XLIV
Thailand: Grain Area, Yields, and Production
(25-Year Averages and Growth Rates, 1961-1986)

Crop	Area		Yield		Production	
	Average %	% Increase	Average MT	% Increase	Average MT	% Increase
Cereal Grains	100	2.5	1.9	0.7	17,191	3.2
Rice	88	1.9	1.9	0.6	14,750	2.5
Maize	11	7.5	2.2	0.8	2,272	8.3

Note: Average area is the share of a grain in terms of total cultivated area
of cereals; average yield is in metric tons/ha; average MT is in thousands
All growth rates are annualized averages for whole 1961-1986 period.

Table XLV
Thailand: Domestic Consumption and Export of Selected Food Crops
(Annual Growth Rates, 1967-1980)

Commodity	% Increase in Consumption	% Increase in Exports
Rice	2.5	6.4
Maize	26.0[a]	6.0[a]
Sugar	6.8	34.4
Cassava		
Chips/pellets	−	17.6
Flour	8.2	−

Note: [a]Figures are for 1967-1976.

Table XLVI
Indonesia: Grain Area, Yields, and Production
(25-Year Averages and Growth Rates, 1961-1986)

	Area		Yield		Production	
Crop	Average %	% Increase	Average MT	% Increase	Average MT	% Increase
Cereal Grains	100	1.2	2.3	3.6	26,334	4.8
Rice	75	1.5	2.7	3.6	22,911	5.2
Maize	25	0.2	1.2	2.8	3,407	3.0

Note: Average area is the share of a grain in terms of total cultivated area
of cereals; average yield is in metric tons/ha; average MT is in thousands.
All growth rates are annualized averages for whole 1961-1986 period.

Table XLVII
China: Area, Yield, and Production of Selected Cereals & Grains
(25-Year Average Levels and Growth, 1961-1986)

Crop	Area		Yield		Production	
	Average %	Growth	Average MT	Growth	Average MT	Growth
Cereal Grains	96	0.0	2.5	4.7	229,968	4.7
Rice	35	0.8	3.7	3.1	119,879	4.4
Wheat	29	0.8	1.6	6.6	44,606	7.6
Maize	19	1.1	2.4	4.6	43,067	5.7
Sorghum	5	-4.9	1.9	5.3	7,701	-0.1
Millet	6	-3.2	1.3	3.3	5,532	-3.3
Barley	2	-5.7	1.7	3.9	3,259	-2.1
Oats	1	-3.1	1.3	0.9	562	-1.7

Note: Average area is the share of a grain in terms of total cultivated area
of cereals; average yield is in metric tons/ha; average MT is in thousands.
All growth rates are annualized averages for whole 1961-1986 period.

Table XLVIII
Substitution of Grains in Production in China, 1961-1985
(As a Percentage of Total Grain Area)

	Increasing Grains			Decreasing Grains	
	1961-1965	1981-1985		1961-1965	1981-1985
Rice	31	36	Sorghum	7	3
Maize	16	20	Barley	4	1
Wheat	27	32	Millet	8	4

 Appendixes

Cultivated Grain Area by Country, 1961–1986
(25-Year Averages and Growth Rates)

Region and Country	All Crops Area	Growth	All Cereals Area[a]	Growth	Sorghum Area[b]	Growth	Maize Area[b]	Growth	Wheat Area[b]	Growth	Rice Area[b]	Growth	Barley Area[b]	Growth	Millet Area[b]	Growth
Latin America																
Argentina	100	0.2	73	0.5	15	3.7	27	0.7	45	0.7	1	3.7	3	-7.6	2	-1.1
Brazil	100	0.0	52	2.5	0	0.0	59	2.2	11	5.3	28	1.9	0	2.6	0	—[d]
Colombia	100	0.0	43	0.3	10	19.6	54	-0.8	5	-4.9	27	1.4	4	-2.8	0	—
Mexico	100	0.0	69	1.2	11	1.3	75	0.4	9	1.6	2	1.5	3	-0.1	0	—
Peru	100	0.1	50	0.1	45	0.7	16	-2.5	16	4.2	20	-2.8	2	2.8	0	—
Venezuela	100	0.0	51	2.4	12	26.7	69	0.0	0	0.0	19	3.6	0	—	0	—
Northern Africa and the Middle East																
Algeria	100	0.3	91	0.0	0	-6.3	0	-2.7	69	-0.5	0	-6.0	28	0.5	0	—
Egypt	100	-0.1	66	0.1	—[c]	—	38	0.6	28	-0.7	12	0.6	3	0.2	10	-1.0
Morocco	100	0.8	91	1.1	2	-6.1	10	-0.6	41	1.0	0	-0.1	45	1.7	0	-5.0
Turkey	100	0.6	85	0.1	0	—	5	-0.5	66	0.8	1	-0.2	21	0.8	0	-7.1
Western Africa																
Burkina Faso	100	0.8	76	0.7	51	0.6	7	-0.5	0	—	2	-4.0	0	—	39	1.3
Nigeria	100	1.3	51	-0.3	46	-0.3	9	-2.7	0	3.3	4	6.1	0	—	41	-0.3
Eastern and Southern Africa																
Ethiopia	100	-0.8	72	-0.8	19	0.2	16	0.2	14	-1.1	0	—	18	0.0	5	-0.2
Kenya	100	0.1	63	0.7	11	-0.1	76	0.9	7	1.2	1	5.3	1	-2.6	4	-1.9
South Africa	100	2.4	88	0.7	5	0.2	68	-0.1	22	2.3	0	—	0	0.5	1	3.9
Sudan	100	4.8	71	5.2	68	5.1	1	2.5	4	8.2	0	9.5	0	—	27	0.1
Tanzania	100	0.7	50	4.0	20	6.1	57	3.3	25	0.1	95	0.7	0	16.3	1	22.9
Zimbabwe	100	2.3	83	1.5	11	3.0	63	2.4	1	17.8	0	-6.3	0	10.3	24	-2.3

Southern Asia																
Bangladesh	100	87	0.5	0.9	0	-2.2	0	-7.5	2	10.0	97	0.7	0	-5.2	0	—
India	100	68	0.6	0.5	17	-0.6	6	1.1	18	2.5	38	0.6	2	-3.7	20	-0.5
Southeastern Asia																
Indonesia	100	77	0.8	1.2	0	-14.7	25	0.2	0	—	75	1.5	0	—	0	—
Philippines	100	88	1.2	1.3	0	—	45	2.6	0	—	55	0.3	0	—	0	—
Thailand	100	86	3.1	2.5	1	11.0	11	7.5	0	—	88	1.9	0	—	0	—
Eastern Asia																
China	100	74	0.3	0.0	5	-4.9	19	1.1	29	0.8	35	0.8	2	-5.7	6	-3.2
USSR	100	80	-0.1	0.0	0	3.7	3	-1.9	52	-1.1	0	7.4	22	2.6	3	-1.8

Note:

[a] The area of cereals is the average percentage of total cultivated cropland.

[b] The area of each grain is the average percentage of total cultivated cereal land.

[c] FAO data for sorghum in Egypt appear to be listed as intercropped with millet.

[d] A dash means that production of this grain is negligible or nonexistent. Oats and rye are omitted from this table because data on their cultivation is scant.

Grain Yields by Country, 1961–1986
(25-Year Averages and Growth Rates)

Region and Country	All Cereals Average Yield	% Growth	Wheat Average Yield	% Growth	Maize Average Yield	% Growth	Sorghum Average Yield	% Growth	Rice Average Yield	% Growth	Barley Average Yield	% Growth	Millet Average Yield	% Growth
Latin America														
Argentina	1.9	2.3	1.5	1.1	2.6	3.0	2.3	2.5	3.6	0.4	1.3	1.7	1.3	0.6
Brazil	1.4	1.1	0.9	3.3	1.5	1.3	1.8	-1.5	0.5	1.0	2.6	0.9	1.7	—[a]
Colombia	2.0	2.9	1.2	2.5	1.3	1.1	2.3	0.7	3.5	3.7	1.7	-0.5	—	—
Mexico	1.7	3.3	3.2	3.5	1.4	2.7	2.9	1.7	2.8	1.6	1.3	3.9	1.0	1.4
Peru	1.8	2.2	1.0	0.6	1.7	1.6	2.8	2.4	4.2	0.5	0.9	0.4	0.9	-0.6
Venezuela	1.6	2.8	0.4	-1.0	1.3	2.9	1.6	-0.7	2.4	2.3	—	—	—	—
Northern Africa and the Middle East														
Algeria	0.6	1.2	0.6	1.0	1.1	2.1	1.4	3.2	2.9	-1.1	0.6	1.9	0.6	0.1
Egypt	3.9	1.5	3.1	1.6	3.7	2.4	3.8	0.2	5.4	0.6	2.5	0.0	—	—
Morocco	0.9	1.6	1.0	2.4	0.7	0.0	0.7	0.4	4.1	-0.5	0.9	1.1	0.8	1.3
Turkey	1.5	2.3	1.5	2.4	2.0	3.6	—	—	4.3	0.7	1.6	1.9	1.5	2.2
Western Africa														
Burkina Faso	0.5	1.8	0.5	1.8	0.7	2.0	0.6	1.8	1.1	4.2	—	—	—	—
Nigeria	0.9	1.7	2.0	1.3	1.2	3.7	0.9	1.0	1.6	2.7	—	—	—	—
Eastern and Southern Africa														
Ethiopia	0.9	1.7	0.9	2.2	1.3	2.5	1.0	1.1	—	—	0.9	1.7	0.7	1.3
Kenya	1.5	0.7	1.6	2.3	1.5	0.8	1.0	-1.7	4.3	0.2	1.4	2.1	0.8	7.4
South Africa	1.3	0.6	1.0	1.7	1.5	0.7	1.2	2.7	2.0	2.0	1.2	3.5	0.4	-5.5
Sudan	0.7	-2.3	1.2	-0.5	0.6	-1.7	0.8	-2.1	0.9	-2.8	0.3	—	—	—
Tanzania	0.9	1.1	1.3	2.1	1.0	1.7	0.7	0.4	1.3	0.5	1.1	0.6	—	—
Zimbabwe	1.2	2.2	3.8	5.5	1.5	1.8	0.5	-0.8	1.0	0.3	4.3	3.6	—	—

Southern Asia														
Bangladesh	1.8	1.3	1.2	5.5	0.8	0.2	0.8	-3.0	1.8	1.3	0.6	0.4	—	—
	1.2	2.3	1.3	3.6	1.1	1.3	0.6	1.4	1.7	1.7	1.0	1.8	—	—
India														
Southeastern Asia														
Indonesia	2.3	3.6	—	—	1.2	2.8	—	—	2.7	3.8	—	—	—	—
Philippines	1.4	2.6	—	—	0.9	2.3	1.4	-20.1	1.8	3.3	—	—	—	—
Thailand	1.9	0.7	—	—	2.2	0.8	1.6	-2.4	1.9	0.6	—	—	—	—
Eastern Asia														
China	2.5	4.7	1.6	6.6	2.4	4.6	1.9	5.3	3.7	3.6	1.7	3.9	1.3	0.9
USSR	1.4	2.2	1.4	2.2	2.8	1.7	1.2	2.6	3.5	2.4	1.4	1.7	1.3	3.2
Developing Market	3.0	2.3	2.2	2.1	4.8	2.7	3.7	1.5	5.5	1.0	2.7	1.7	2.0	1.4

Note: A dash means that production of this grain is negligible or nonexistent. Oats and rye are omitted from this table because the data on yields is scant.

Notes

1. In some cases, the use of grain may even differ from region to region within a country; such variations are not considered in this book.

2. We would expect a more detailed study of Colombia by a collaborative national research group to analyze the changes in the cultivation of roots and tubers, which are clearly an important food source for poor people. They may have become even more important in recent years as maize availablity has declined.

3. See Thomas (1985) for a detailed study of the impact of macroeconomic policies on agriculture.

4. Between 1969–1971 and 1979–1981, the retail price of maize rose 744% as opposed to 599% for rice and 632% for wheat (Bolling 1987).

5. The modernization of Mexico's agriculture and the role of sorghum in that process has been amply documented and will be only briefly reviewed here. See, for example, Barkin and DeWalt (1988); DeWalt (1985a); Barkin and Suárez (1985); Hewitt de Alcántara (1976).

6. See, for example, Feder (1977) and Rama and Vigorito (1979) for an account of the expansion of these transnational industries.

7. Because of the importance of noncereal staples in Brazil, a full comprehension of recent changes in food production must include an analysis of these important crops, as well as the traditional grains.

8. The data presented here are adapted from Graham et al. (1987:8). Our analysis relies on the in-country data compiled by the Fundação Instituto Brasileiro de Geografía e Estatística (FIBGE) because it appears more reliable than the FAO data, particularly with respect to the relationship between cereal and noncereal production, which the FAO data show to be relatively constant. Several studies using different methodologies and based on the FIBGE data show that export crops have expanded dramatically in relation to cereal crops (Homem de Melo 1986; Romeiro 1987; and Gray 1982). The FAO and FIBGE data are more consistent with respect to the changing composition of grain

production—for example, in the relative increase in wheat and decrease in maize production—during the period in question.

9. Gray estimates that it takes between 235,000 and 525,000 hectares of cane to produce 1 billion liters of ethanol, depending on plant yields and the efficiency of the distilling process.

10. For a case study of government intervention in favor of export-oriented commercial enterprises in the Amazonia and the consequent increase in land concentration, landlessness, regional food deficiencies, and rural violence, see Hall (1987).

11. See Romeiro (1987:88) for a fuller account of the proletarianization of the rural work force.

12. The calculation is based on domestic production minus exports, plus imports; seeds, losses, and changes in stocks were not included for lack of annual data (Homem de Melo 1986:48).

13. Khaldi defines the region's countries as oil-exporting, labor-exporting, or food-producing, according to the primary source of economic earnings, even though all may have some oil, export some workers, and have significant agricultural production. The oil states include Algeria, Iran, Iraq, Kuwait, Libya, Oman, and Saudi Arabia; labor exporters include Egypt, Jordan, Lebanon, the People's Democratic Republic of Yemen, and the Yemen Arab Republic; Afghanistan, Cyprus, Morocco, Sudan, Syria, Tunisia, and Turkey are the region's major food producers.

14. Khaldi's study is based on FAO supply utilization tapes, which shed light on some structural changes that are not evident from the production data we used. However, the aggregate regional-level analysis also reveals certain important country variations, thereby pointing out the need for country-by-country reviews such as those included in this book.

15. On a regional level, the growth in consumption of feed versus food staples in northern Africa is second only to the growth in Mexico and Central America. Between 1966 and 1980, feed use of staples grew at an annual rate of 6.9% (versus 7.5% in Mexico and Central America). At the same time, food use of staples grew at 3.9% (Paulino 1986:26).

16. A further study is warranted of the impact on barley production of government policies to promote food self-sufficiency.

17. It would be worthwhile to review data from the 1950s to check whether the increase in wheat cultivation relative to barley was a long-term trend that was reversed in the mid-1960s, or whether the dip was a minor aberration.

18. The statistics in Table XXIV are based on the FAO data, but a comparison with in-country data shows little variation. The exceptions are sorghum and millet. While the FAO reports an average of 10% of the grain area in millet, the Egyptian Ministry of Agriculture reports approximately the same percentage in sorghum. It is assumed for purposes of this book that the sorghum and millet are intercropped, a common practice in northern Africa.

19. According to Richards (1982:247), in the late 1970s farmers received the following percentages of international prices for agricultural commodities: cotton, 49%; wheat, 69%; rice, 75%; sorghum, 78%; maize, 69%; berseem clover, 100%; milk, 100%; meat, 180%, owing to a high government subsidy.

20. See, for example, Goueli (1981:143).

21. Worker remittances surpassed cotton as the primary source of foreign exchange in the 1970s. Remittances rose from less than $100 million in 1973 to $2.5 billion in 1980, and to almost $3.5 billion in 1983 (Bredhal 1985).

22. The study was based on a random sample of 1,000 households in 18 villages in Egypt.

23. By contrast, animal products are not an important part of the Nigerian diet.

24. Statement by the then new head of state, Major General Muhammadu Buhari, May 1984, quoted in Andrae and Beckman (1985:2).

25. The exception to this is Ethiopia, where cultivated cereal land in general declined, and increasing yields compensated for lost acreage to some extent.

26. A more detailed study of Zimbabwe's agriculture would thus need to examine why maize has supplanted sorghum and millet even in the communal areas: Is it due to governmental price policy, higher relative yields, preferences in consumption, or other factors?

27. By contrast, China's rice yields averaged 3.7 kg/ha and rose at 3.6% per year.

28. See, for example, Nicholson (1984:570), Agrawal (1980:142–172), and Spitz (1987).

29. This section is based on the FAO data and complemented by Nestel's (1985) study.

30. Our analysis covers 96% of all cultivated land in cereal production, including rice, wheat, maize, sorghum, barley, oats, millet, and rye. It accounts for an average of 74% of all cultivated land in China.

31. These percentages were calculated on the basis of three-year beginning and end point averages.

32. Our research also shows that in most cases the attempt to promote specialization in agricultural production to exploit a country's comparative advantage frequently violates the very precepts by which the model is developed. Specifically, the move toward specialization often idles land and wrests people from rural production, while not offering alternative productive uses for either.

33. The International Food Policy Research Institute (IFPRI) has conducted a series of case studies analyzing the impact of price policies on food production and consumption; see, for example, Cavallo and Mundlak (1982) and von Braun and de Haen (1983). See also Barkin and Suárez (1985).

34. This issue was recently raised in a debate that raged through the pages of *Tijdschrift voor sociaalwteenschappelijk onderzoek can de landbouw* (Agricultural University at Wageningen, the Netherlands) during 1987–1988 between Alan Matthews, Rod Tyers, and Kym Anders, on the one hand, and Jerrie de Hoogh, on the other. At issue was the impact of the changing international division of labor in world agriculture between the developed and the less developed countries. The first group in some way contributed to the finding of the World Bank's *World Development Report 1986* that liberalization of international agricultural trade would bring substantial benefits to the Third World (as well as to the advanced countries). De Hoogh, in contrast, argued that because technical development in the rich countries is quite insensitive to price changes, the secular increase in productivity vitiates this conclusion. He added—more tellingly—that low world prices are an obstruction to agricultural development in the poorer parts of the world; therefore, it is essential—from the perspective of the development of these countries—for them to establish systems that protect the healthy development of their agriculture.

35. Of course, the advanced industrial countries do not have this ability either. Economists often point out that in this imperfect world, it is often preferable to adopt policies that are not quite as efficient as the ideal but have a more equitable distributional impact.

Bibliography

Agrawal, A.N. 1980. *Indian Agriculture: Problems, Progress, Prospects.* New Delhi: Vikas Publishing House.

Alderman, Harold, and Joachim von Braun. 1984. *The Effects of the Egyptian Food Ration and Subsidy System on Income Distribution and Consumption.* Research Report No. 45. Washington, DC: IFPRI, July.

Ames, C.W., and Paul A. Wojtkowski. 1987/1988. "Feast or Famine: Projections of Food Supply, Demand, and Human Nutrition for Five African Countries." *Journal of African Studies* 14, no. 4.

Andrae, Gunilla, and Bjorn Beckman. 1985. *The Wheat Trap.* London: Zed Books.

Arroyo, Gonzalo, S. Gomes de Almeida, and J.M. von der Weid. 1980. "Empresas transnacionales y agricultura en América Latina." *Revista Estudio del Tercer Mundo* 3 (2): 143-202.

Barkin, David. 1981. "El uso de la tierra agrícola en México." *Problemas Del Desarrollo* 47/48: 59–78.

_____. 1982. "The Impact of Agribusiness on Rural Development." In *Current Perspectives in Social Theory,* Vol. 3, ed. S. McNall. Greenwich, CT: JAI Press.

_____. 1985. "Global Proletarianization." In *The Americas in the New International Division of Labor,* ed. S. Sanderson. New York: Holmes and Meier.

_____. 1987. "SAM and Seeds." In *Food Policy in Mexico: The Search for Self-Sufficiency,* ed. J. Austin and G. Esteva. Ithaca, NY: Cornell University Press.

_____, and Billie R. DeWalt. 1988. "Sorghum and the Mexican Food Crisis." *Latin American Research Review* 23, no. 3:30–59.

_____, and Blanca Suárez. 1985. *El fin de la autosuficiencia alimentaria.* Mexico City: Editorial Océano and Centro de Ecodesarrollo.

Barzelay, Michael, and Scott Pearson. 1982. "The Efficiency of Producing Alcohol for Energy in Brazil." *Economic Development and Cultural Change* 31, no. 1 (October): 131–144.

Billing, K. J. 1985. *Zimbabwe and the CGIAR Centers: A Study in Their Collaboration in Agricultural Research.* Washington, DC: World Bank.

Binns, J. A. 1986. "After the Drought: Field Observations from Mali and Burkina Faso." *Geography* 71, no. 3.

Bolling, H. Christine. 1987. *Colombia: An Export Market Profile.* Foreign Agricultural Economic Report No. 225. Washington, DC: USDA.

Bothmani, Isaac B. 1984/1985. "The Food Crisis in East and Central Africa with Special Reference to Kenya, Malawi, Tanzania, and Zambia." *Journal of African Studies* 11, no. 4.

Bredahl, Maury E. 1985. *Macroeconomic Policy and Agricultural Development: Concepts and Case Studies of Egypt, Morocco, and Jordan.* Columbia, MO: University of Missouri International Agriculture Series.

Carmona, Fernando, *et al.* 1983. *El milagro mexicano.* Mexico City: Editorial Nuestro Tiempo.

Carroll, Jane. 1987. "Kenya: Economy." In *Africa South of the Sahara.* London: Europa.

Cavallo, Domingo, and Yair Mundlak. 1982. *Agriculture and Economic Growth in an Open Economy: The Case of Argentina.* Research Report No. 36. Washington, DC: IFPRI, December.

Centro de Ecodesarrollo and Fundación Friedrich Naumann. 1988. *¿Producimos para la desnutrición?* Mexico: Centro de Ecodesarrollo.

Chiriboga, Manuel, ed. 1988. *El problema agrario en el Ecuador.* Quito, Ecuador: ILDIS.

CIMMYT. 1984. *1984 CIMMYT Maize Facts and Trends. Report Two: An Analysis of Changes in Third World Food and Feed Uses of Maize.* Mexico City: CIMMYT.

_____. 1985. *1985 CIMMYT World Wheat Facts and Trends. Report Three: A Discussion of Selected Wheat Marketing and Pricing Issues in Developing Countries.* Mexico City: CIMMYT.

Couriel, Alberto. 1984. "Poverty and Underemployment in Latin America." *CEPAL Review* 24: 39–62.

Denslow, David, and William Tyler. 1984. "Perspectives on Poverty and Income Inequality in Brazil." *World Development* 12 (October): 1019–1028.

DeWalt, Billie. 1983. "The Cattle Are Eating the Forest." *Bulletin of the Atomic Scientists* 39:18-23.

_____. 1985a. "Mexico's Second Green Revolution: Food For Feed." *Mexican Studies/Estudios Mexicanos* 1, no. 1:29–60.

_____. 1985b. "Un panorama de la producción del maíz y sorgo en el hemisferio occidental." In *El sorgo en sistemas de producción en América Latina,* ed. C. Paul and B. R. Dewalt. Mexico City:

INTSORMIL/ICRISAT/CIMMYT.

———. 1985c. "Microcosmic and Macrocosmic Processes of Agrarian Change in Southern Honduras: the Cattle Are Eating The Forest." In *Micro and Macro Levels of Analysis in Anthropology: Issues in Theory and Research*, ed. Billie R. DeWalt and Pertti J. Pelto. Boulder, CO: Westview Press: 165–186.

———. 1986. "Economic Assistance in Central America: Development or Impoverishment?" *Cultural Survival Quarterly* 10:14–18.

———, and David Barkin. 1985. "El sorgo y la crisis alimentaria mexicana." In *El sorgo en sistemas de producción en América Latina*, ed. C. Paul and B. R. Dewalt. Mexico City: INTSORMIL/ICRISAT/CIMMYT.

———, and David Barkin. 1987. "Seeds of Change: The Effects of Hybrid Sorghum and Agricultural Modernization in Mexico." In *Technology and Social Change*, 2d. ed., eds. Russell H. Bernard and Pertti J. Pelto. Prospect Heights, IL: Waveland Press.

———, et al. 1987. "Agrarian Reform and Small Farmer Welfare: Evidence from Four Mexican Communities." *Food and Nutrition Bulletin* 9, no. 3:46–52.

Dorosh, Paul A., et al. 1987. "Introduction to the Corn Economy of Indonesia." In *The Corn Economy of Indonesia*, ed. C. Peter Timmer. Ithaca, NY: Cornell University Press.

Elías, Victor J. 1985. *Government Expenditures on Agriculture and Agricultural Growth in Latin America*. Research Report No. 50. Washington, DC: IFPRI, October.

Feder, Ernst. 1977. *Strawberry Imperialism: An Inquiry into the Mechanism of Dependency in Mexico*. The Hague: Institute of Social Studies.

Fox, Roger. 1979. *Brazil's Minimum Price Policy and the Agricultural Sector of Northeast Brazil*. Research Report No. 9. Washington, DC: IFPRI, June.

Franke, Richard, and Barbara Chasin. 1980. *Seeds of Famine: Ecological Destruction and the Development Dilemma in the West African Sahel*. Montclair, NJ: Allanheld Osmun.

García García, Jorge. 1981. "The Nature of Food Insecurity in Colombia." In *Food Security for Developing Countries*, ed. Alberto Valdes. Boulder, CO: Westview Press.

García, Rolando. 1981. *Drought and Man*, Vol. 1: *Nature Pleads Not Guilty*. London: Pergamon Press.

Gardner, George R., and John Parker. 1985. *Egypt: An Export Market Profile*. FAER Report No. 215. Washington, DC: USDA.

George, Susan. 1977. *How The Other Half Dies*. Montclair, NJ: Allanheld Osmun.

Gervais, Myriam. 1984. "Peasants and Capital in Upper Volta." In *The Politics of Agriculture in Tropical Africa*, ed. Jonathan Baker. Beverly Hills and London: Sage.

Gómez, Arturo. 1985. *The Philippines and the CGIAR Centers: A Study in Their Collaboration in Agricultural Research.* Washington, DC: World Bank.

González B., Bernardo. 1986. "Evaluación de la producción de cereales en Venezuela: aspectos para el futuro." In Comisión Coordinadora de Investigaciones en Alimentos y Nutrición, *Los cereales en el patrón alimentario del venezolano.* Caracas, Venezuela: FUNDACAVENDES.

Goueli, Ahmed. 1981. "The Food Security Program in Egypt." In *Food Security in Developing Countries,* ed. Alberto Valdes. Boulder, CO: Westview Press.

Graham, Douglas, *et al.* 1987. "Thirty Years of Agricultural Growth in Brazil: Crop Performance, Regional Profile, and Recent Policy Review." *Economic Development and Cultural Change* 36, no. 1 (October): 1–34.

Gray, Cheryl Williamson. 1982. *Food Consumption Parameters for Brazil.* Report No. 32. Washington, DC: IFPRI, September.

Hall, Anthony L. 1987. "Agrarian Crisis in Brazilian Amazonia: The Grande Carajas Programme." *Journal of Development Studies* 23, no. 4: 522–552.

Hall, Lana L. 1985. "U.S. Food Aid and the Agricultural Development of Brazil and Colombia, 1954–1973." In *Food, Politics, and Society in Latin America,* ed. John C. Super and Thomas C. Wright. Lincoln and London: University of Nebraska Press.

Hecht, Susanna B. 1985. "Environment, Development and Politics: Capital Accumulation and the Livestock Sector in Eastern Amazonia." *World Development* 14, no. 4 (1985):663–684.

Helmsing, J. 1986. *Firms, Farms, and the State in Colombia.* Boston: Allen and Unwin.

Herdt, Robert, *et al.* 1985. *The Rice Economy of Asia.* Washington, DC: Resources for the Future.

Hewitt de Alcántara, Cynthia. 1976. *Modernizing Mexican Agriculture.* Geneva: United Nations Research Institute for Social Development.

Hodgkinson, Edith. 1987. "Burkina Faso: Economy." In *Africa South of the Sahara.* London: Europa Publications.

Homem de Melo, Fernando. 1986. *Brazil and the CGIAR Centers: A Study in Their Collaboration in Agricultural Research.* Washington, DC: World Bank.

_____. 1987. "Export-oriented Agricultural Growth: The Case of Brazil." World Employment Programme Research. WEP 10-6/WP87. Geneva: International Labour Organisation, September.

House, Leland R. 1985. *A Guide to Sorghum Breeding,* 2d ed. Patancheru, India: International Crops Research Institute for the Semi-arid Tropics.

Huddleston, Barbara. 1987. "Trends in Trade and Food Aid." In *Food Policy: Integrating Supply, Distribution, and Consumption,* ed. J. Price Gittinger, Joanne Leslie, and Caroline Hoisington. EDI Series in Economic Development. Baltimore and London: Johns Hopkins University Press.

Interamerican Development Bank (IDB). 1986. *Economic and Social Progress in Latin America.* Washington, DC:IDB.

Isarangkura, Rungrung. 1986. *Thailand and the CGIAR Centers: A Study in Their Collaboration in Agricultural Research.* Washington, DC: World Bank.

Jabara, Cathy. 1985. "Agricultural Pricing Policy in Kenya." *World Development* 13, no. 5.

Jaffé Carbonell, W., and Harry Rothman. 1977. "An Implicit Food Policy: Wheat Consumption Changes in Venezuela." *Food Policy* 11.

Jennings, Bruce H. 1988. *Foundations of International Agricultural Research.* Boulder, Co.: Westview Press.

Jennings, Peter R., and James H. Cock. 1977. "Centres of Origin of Crops and Their Productivity." *Economic Botany* 31:51–54.

Khaldi, Nabil. 1984. *Evolving Food Gaps in the Middle East/North Africa: Prospects and Policy Implications.* Research Report No. 47. Washington, DC: IFPRI, December.

Kolko, Joyce. 1988. *Restructuring the World Economy.* New York: Pantheon Books.

Konjing, Khaisri, and Madee Veerakitpanich. 1985. "Food Consumption and Nutrition in Thailand." In *Food Policy Analysis in Thailand,* ed. Theodore Panaytou. Bangkok: Allied Printers.

Koppel, Bruce. 1987. "Agrarian Problems and Agrarian Reform: Opportunity or Irony?" In *Rebuilding a Nation: Philippine Challenges and American Policy,* ed. Carle Lande. Washington, DC: Washington Institute Press.

Kumar, Shubh K. 1987. "The Nutrition Situation and Its Food Policy Links." In *Accelerating Food Production in Sub-Saharan Africa,* ed. John Mellor, Christopher Delgado, and Malcolm Blackie. Baltimore and London: Johns Hopkins University Press.

Leamer, Edward E. 1984. *Sources of International Comparative Advantage: Theory and Evidence.* Cambridge, MA: Massachusetts Institute of Technology.

Lipton, Michael, with Richard Longhurst. 1988. *New Seeds and Poor People.* Baltimore, MD: Johns Hopkins University Press.

Little, Peter, and Michael Horowitz. 1987. "Subsistence Crops Are Cash Crops: Some Comments with Reference to Eastern Africa." *Human Organization* 46, no.3.

Mabbs-Zeno, Carl. 1986. *Nigeria: An Export Market Profile.* FAER Report No. 218.Washington, DC: USDA.

Mahapatra, Ishwar Chandra, *et al.* 1986. *India and the International Crops Research Institute for the Semi-Arid Tropics (ICRISAT).* Washington, DC: World Bank.

May, Peter H. 1988. "Northeast Brazilian Agriculture: An Overview." January 1988.

McMillan, Della. 1985. "A Resettlement Scheme in Upper Volta." Ph.D. thesis, Evanston, IL: Northwestern University.

———. 1987. "The Social Impacts of Planned Settlement in Burkina

Faso." In *Drought and Hunger in Sub-Saharan Africa,* ed. Michael Glantz. London: Cambridge University Press.

Mink, Stephen D. 1987."Corn in the Livestock Economy." In *The Corn Economy of Indonesia,* ed. C. Peter Timmer. Ithaca, NY: Cornell University Press.

Monteverde, Gerhard, and Stephen Mink. 1987. "Household Corn Consumption." In *The Corn Economy of Indonesia,* ed. C. Peter Timmer. Ithaca, NY: Cornell University Press.

Moore Lappé, Francis, and Joseph Collins. 1977. *Food First: Beyond the Myth of Scarcity.* New York: Houghton Mifflin.

Nestel, Barry. 1985. *Indonesia and the CGIAR Centers: A Study of Their Collaboration in Agricultural Research.* Washington, DC: World Bank.

Niblo, Stephen R. 1988. The *Impact of War: Mexico and World War II.* Melbourne, Australia: La Trobe University Institute of Latin American Studies.

Nicholson, Norman K. 1984. "Landholding, Agricultural Modernization, and Local Institutions in India." *Economic Development and Cultural Change* 32.

Panaytou, Theodore. 1985. *Food Policy Analysis in Thailand.* Bangkok: Allied Printers.

Panpiemras, Kosit, and Somchai Krusuansombat. 1985. "Seasonal Migration and Employment in Thailand." In *Food Policy Analysis in Thailand,* ed. Theodore Panaytou. Bangkok: Allied Printers.

Paulino, Leonardo A. 1986. *Food in the Third World: Past Trends and Projections to 2000.* IFPRI Report No. 52. Washington, DC: IFPRI, June.

Paz Silva, Luis J. 1986. *Peru and the CGIAR Centers: A Study of Their Collaboration in Agricultural Research.* CGIAR Study Paper No. 12. Washington, DC: World Bank.

Pearse, Andrew. 1980. *Seeds of Plenty, Seeds of Want.* Oxford: Oxford University Press.

Pitner, John B., *et al.* 1954. *El cultivo del sorgo.* Mexico City: Programa Cooperativo de Agricultura de la Secretaría de Agricultura y Ganadería de México y la Fundación Rockefeller.

Puapanichya, Kumpol, and Theodore Panaytou. 1985. "Output Supply and Input Demand in Rice and Upland Crop Production." In *Food Policy Analysis in Thailand,* ed. Theodore Panaytou. Bangkok: Allied Printers.

Radwan, Samir, and Eddy Lee. 1986. *Agrarian Change in Egypt: An Anatomy of Rural Poverty.* London: Croom Helm.

Rama, Ruth, and Raul Vigorito. 1979. *El Complejo de frutas y legumbres en México.* Mexico City: Editorial Nueva Imagen.

Redclift, Michael R. 1981. "Development Policy Making in Mexico: The Sistema Alimentario Mexicano (SAM)." Working Papers in U.S.-Mexican Studies No. 24. La Jolla: University of California at San Diego.

Reig, Nicolas. 1980. "La economía ganadera mundial: hegemonía de Estados Unidos y nuevas tendencias." *Revista Estudios del Tercer Mundo* 3 (2): 73-98.

Richards, Alan. 1982. *Egypt's Agricultural Development, 1800–1980: Technical and Social Change.* Boulder, CO: Westview Press.

Robinson, Joan. 1979. *Aspects of Development and Underdevelopment.* Cambridge: Cambridge University Press.

Rockefeller Foundation. 1957. *Mexican Agricultural Program, 1956–1957: Director's Annual Report.* New York: Rockefeller Foundation.

Romeiro, Ademar Ribeiro. 1987. "Alternative Developments in Brazil." In *The Green Revolution Revisited,* ed. Bernhard Glasser. London: Allen and Unwin.

Roy, Sajit. 1987. "Agrarian Crisis and Technology in Nigeria." *African Quarterly* 25, nos. 1–2.

San Martin, P., and B. Pelegrini. 1984. *Cerrados: uma ocupacão japonesa no campo.* Rio de Janeiro: CODECRI.

Sarma, J.S. 1986. *Cereal Feed Use in the Third World: Past Trends and Projections to 2000.* Research Report No. 57. Washington, DC: IFPRI, December.

Scobie, Grant. 1981. *Government Policy and Food Imports: The Case of Wheat in Egypt.* Research Report No. 29. Washington, DC: IFPRI, December.

_____. 1983. *Food Subsidies in Egypt: Their Impact on Foreign Exchange and Trade.* Research Report No. 40. Washington, DC: IFPRI, August.

Sen, A. 1981. *Poverty and Famines: An Essay on Entitlement and Deprivation.* Oxford: Clarendon Press.

Shopo, Thomas D. 1987. *The Political Economy of Hunger and Malnutrition in Zimbabwe.* Harare, Zimbabwe: Institute for Development Studies.

Smil, Vaclav. 1985. "Eating Better: Farming Reforms and Food in China." *Current History* (September): 248–251, 273–274.

Suárez, Blanca, and G. Rodriguez. 1984. "Agroindustria y patrón de desarrollo en América Latina." *Economía de América Latina* 12 (2do. semestre): 109–126.

Suárez, Blanca, and R. Vigorito. 1981/2. "Capital extranjero y complejos agro-alimentarios en América Latina: Historia y estrategia." *Revista Latino-Americana de Economía* 12 (47-48): 151-196.

Spitz, Pierre. 1987. "The Green Revolution Re-examined in India." In *The Green Revolution Revisited,* ed. Bernhard Glasser. London: Allen and Unwin: 56–75.

Temu, Peter. 1984. *Marketing, Board Pricing, and Storage Policy with Particular Reference to Maize in Tanzania.* New York: Vantage Press.

Teubal, Miguel. 1987. "Internationalization of Capital and Agroindustrial Complexes: Their Impact on Latin American Agriculture." *Latin American Perspectives* 54, 14(3).

Thomas, Vinod. 1985. *Linking Macroeconomic and Agricultural Policies for Adjustment with Growth: The Colombian Experience.* Baltimore and London: Johns Hopkins University Press.

Timmer, C. Peter. 1981. "The Formation of Indonesian Rice Policy: A Historical Perspective." In *Agricultural and Rural Development in Indonesia,* ed. Gary E. Hansen. Boulder, CO: Westview Press.

_____. 1986. *Getting Prices Right: The Scope and Limits of Agricultural Price Policy.* Ithaca, NY: Cornell University Press.

_____. 1987. "Corn in Indonesia's Food Policy." In *The Corn Economy of Indonesia,* ed. C. Peter Timmer. Ithaca, NY: Cornell University Press.

_____, et al. 1983. *Food Policy Analysis.* Baltimore, MD: Johns Hopkins Unviersity Press.

Trairatvorakul, Prasarn. 1984. *The Effects on Income Distribution and Nutrition of Alternative Rice Price Policies in Thailand.* Research Report No. 46. Washington, DC: IFPRI, November.

Vermeer, Donald E. 1983. "Food Sufficiency and Farming in the Future of West Africa: Resurgence of Traditional Agriculture?" *Journal of African Studies* 10, no. 3.

Vigorito, Raul. 1984. *Transnacionalización y desarrollo agropecuario en América Latina.* Madrid: Ediciones Cultura Hispánica.

Vocke, Gary. 1986. "Hybrids Increase Sorghum Production in Developing Countries." World Agriculture: Situation and Outlook Report. Washington, DC: USDA Economic Research Service, WAS-46, December.

Von Braun, Joachim, and Hartwig de Haen. 1983. *The Effects of Food Price and Subsidy Policies on Egyptian Agriculture.* Research Report No. 42. Washington, DC: IFPRI, November.

Von Oppen, M., and P.P. Rao. 1982. "Sorghum Marketing in India." *Sorghum in the Eighties,* Vol. 2. Patancheru, India: ICRISAT, October.

Walker, Kenneth R. 1984. *Food Grain Procurement and Consumption in China.* Cambridge: Cambridge University Press.

Watts, Michael. 1987. "Agriculture and Oil-based Accumulation: Stagnation or Transformation?" In *State, Oil, and Agriculture in Nigeria,* ed. M. Watts. Berkeley: University of California Press.

Witte Wright, Eleanor. 1985. "Food Dependency and Malnutrition in Venezuela, 1958–1974." In *Food, Politics, and Society in Latin America,* ed. John C. Super and Thomas C. Wright. Lincoln and London: University of Nebraska Press.

Wolf, Eric. 1982. *Europe and the People Without History.* Berkeley: University of California Press.

World Bank. 1980. *Indonesia: Employment and Income Distribution in Indonesia.* Washington, DC: World Bank.

_____. 1983. *Agricultural and Livestock Research in Upper Volta: Report on a Mission.* The Hague: FAO-ISNAR.

_____. 1986. *World Development Report 1986.* New York: Oxford

University Press.
Yates, P. Lamartine. 1981. *Mexico's Agricultural Dilemma.* Tucson: University of Arizona Press.
Zinyama, L. M. 1986. "Agricultural Development Policies in the African Farming Areas of Zimbabwe." *Geography* 71, no. 2.

Index

The attainment of food self-sufficiency has been a major goal of developing countries over the past 25 years. Yet, in the 1980s, most of these countries have increased, often dramatically, their dependence on food imports.

Within this context, Barkin, Batt, and DeWalt assess the implications for producer welfare of the dramatic changes in glain production and consumption in developing countries from 1960 to 1985—changes in grains produced, who produces them, who buys them, and to what end. As developing economies are inteFated into the world commodity markets, argue the authors, they tend increasingly toward substitution of grains in production: feed crops for animals displace food crops for people. There is also a corresponding shift from labor-intensive farming to mechanized agriculture. As a result, not only does food dependency increase—as measured by continuing growth in imports and foreign trade imbalance—but nutritional improvements are also forestalled. The authors' analysis of changing patterns of grain cultivation identifies how these lead to substantially altered patterns of nutrition, employment generation, and income distribution.

David Barkin is professor of economics at the Universidad Autonoma Metropolitana, Xochimilco, and director of the Morelia Office of the Centro de Ecodesarrollo, Mexico. Rosemary L. Batt is a doctoral candidate in urban studies and planning at the Massachusetts Institute of Technology. Billie R. DeWalt is professor and chair of the Department of Anthropology at the University of Kentucky, Lexington.